UNLOCK

READING & WRITING SKILLS

2

Richard O'Neill

CAMBRIDGE
UNIVERSITY PRESS

CAMBRIDGE
UNIVERSITY PRESS

University Printing House, Cambridge CB2 8BS, United Kingdom

Cambridge University Press is part of the University of Cambridge.

It furthers the University's mission by disseminating knowledge in the pursuit of education, learning and research at the highest international levels of excellence.

www.cambridge.org
Information on this title: www.cambridge.org/9781107614000

© Cambridge University Press 2014

Content and images which are © Discovery Communications, LLC are reproduced here under license.

First published 2014

Printed in China by Golden Cup Printing Co. Ltd

A catalogue record for this publication is available from the British Library

ISBN 978-1-107-61400-0 Reading and Writing 2 Student's Book with Online Workbook
ISBN 978-1-107-61403-1 Reading and Writing 2 Teacher's Book with DVD
ISBN 978-1-107-68232-0 Listening and Speaking 2 Student's Book with Online Workbook
ISBN 978-1-107-64280-5 Listening and Speaking 2 Teacher's Book with DVD

Additional resources for this publication at www.cambridge.org/unlock

CONTENTS

MAP OF THE BOOK

UNIT	VIDEO	READING	VOCABULARY	
1 PLACES Reading 1: Rise of the megacities (Geography) Reading 2: Homestay holidays (Travel and Tourism)	Life in faraway places	*Key reading skill*: Scanning for numbers Understanding key vocabulary Making predictions Reading for main ideas Reading for detail Scanning to find information Working out meaning Scanning to predict content Making inferences	Vocabulary to describe places (e.g. *exciting, interesting, polluted, noisy, boring*)	
2 FESTIVALS AND CELEBRATIONS Reading 1: Celebrate! (Sociology) Reading 2: Muscat Festival (Cultural Studies)	Festivals: Mongolia	*Key reading skill*: Previewing Understanding key vocabulary Reading for main ideas Reading for detail Recognizing text type Scanning to predict content Recognizing text type	Vocabulary to describe festivals (e.g. *lucky, culture, traditional, history, highlights*)	
3 SCHOOL AND EDUCATION Reading 1: La Masia: the best footballers in the world (Education) Reading 2: My Princeford experience (Education)	A reading class	*Key reading skill*: Skimming Understanding key vocabulary Using visuals to predict content Reading for main ideas Reading for detail Understanding discourse Making inferences Previewing Using your knowledge	Vocabulary to describe education (e.g. *a principal, a lecturer, a lab, a graduate, an office*)	
4 THE INTERNET AND TECHNOLOGY Reading 1: Someone's always watching you online … (Information Technology) Reading 2: Video games (Information Technology)	The rise of social media	*Key reading skill*: Making inferences Scanning to predict content Reading for main ideas Reading for detail Understanding key vocabulary Identifying type	Vocabulary to describe the internet and technology (e.g. *an online game, a computer program, a chat room, internet banking, a smartphone*)	
5 LANGUAGE AND COMMUNICATION Reading 1: Writing systems (Linguistics) Reading 2: Language change: a study guide (Linguistics)	The importance of codes	*Key reading skill*: Reading for main ideas Understanding key vocabulary Using your knowledge Reading for main ideas Reading for detail Recognizing text type Scanning to predict content Making inferences	Vocabulary to describe language and communication (e.g. *sign, symbol, information, money, word*)	

GRAMMAR	CRITICAL THINKING	WRITING
Nouns, verbs and adjectives *Grammar for writing*: • Sentence structure 1: subject + verb • *There is / There are*	• Understand the differences between two texts • Evaluate information using a T-chart • Analyze positives and negatives using a T-chart • Create your own T-chart to organize your ideas	*Academic writing skills*: • Capital letters and full stops *Writing task type*: Write descriptive sentences. *Writing task*: Describe the place where you live. Write about the positives and negatives.
Prepositions of time and place: *on, in, at* Adverbs of frequency *Grammar for writing 2*: • Sentence structure 2: subject and verb order • Prepositional phrases	• Apply your knowledge to a calendar • Evaluate events in your country from an outsider's point of view • Create a spider diagram to organize ideas	*Academic writing skills*: • Paragraph organization 1: organizing sentences into a paragraph *Writing task type*: Write a descriptive paragraph. *Writing task*: Describe a festival or special event.
Education nouns Plural nouns *Grammar for writing*: • Subject pronouns • *because* and *so*	• Remember information from texts • Analyze information in your notes • Create a *wh-* chart to organize information	*Academic writing skills*: • Paragraph organization 2: topic and supporting sentences *Writing task type*: Write a descriptive paragraph. *Writing task*: Describe your education.
Compound nouns Giving opinions *Grammar for writing*: • *and, also* and *too* • *but* and *however*	• Analyze an essay question • Evaluate advantages and disadvantages • Create your own list of advantages and disadvantages	*Academic writing skills*: • Topic sentences *Writing task type*: Write a one-sided opinion paragraph. *Writing task*: The internet has made our lives better. Do you agree or disagree?
Countable and uncountable nouns Articles: *a, an* or no article *Grammar for writing*: • Quantifiers: *some, many, a lot of, a few, a little*	• Evaluate ideas and examples using an ideas map • Create your own ideas and examples/evidence	*Academic writing skills*: • Supporting sentences • Giving examples: *like, such as* and *for example* *Writing task type*: Write a descriptive paragraph. *Writing task*: How is your language different from 50 years ago? Describe the way that people speak and write your language has changed.

UNIT	VIDEO	READING	VOCABULARY	
6 WEATHER AND CLIMATE Reading 1: Extreme weather (Geography) Reading 2: Surviving the Sea of Sand (Environmental Science)	Stormchasers	*Key reading skill*: Using your knowledge to predict content Understanding key vocabulary Reading for main ideas Reading for detail Recognizing text type	Vocabulary to describe temperatures and graphs (e.g. *high, low, rise, drop, an increase, a decrease*)	
7 SPORTS AND COMPETITION Reading 1: Five strange sports (Sports Science) Reading 2: Tough man: a race to the limit (Sports Science)	Sports and competition	*Key reading skill*: Scanning to predict content Understanding key vocabulary Skimming Reading for detail Recognizing text type Previewing Reading for main ideas Understanding discourse Working out meaning	Vocabulary to describe prepositions of movement (e.g. *past, through, across, along, over*)	
8 BUSINESS Reading 1: Are you ready for the world of work? (Human Resources) Reading 2: You can choose your grandma! (Business)	The changing world of business	*Key reading skill*: Working out meaning from context Scanning to predict content Reading for main ideas Reading for detail Working out meaning Identifying the audience Understanding key vocabulary Scanning to predict content Making inferences	Vocabulary to describe business (e.g. *set up, a business partner, an employee, employ, a product*)	
9 PEOPLE Reading 1: Respect! (Sociology) Reading 2: People I admire (Sociology)	Mine rescue	*Key reading skill*: Reading for detail Understanding key vocabulary Scanning to predict content Reading for main ideas Identifying purpose Making inferences	Vocabulary to describe people (e.g. *reliable, talented, patient, sensible, selfish*)	
10 SPACE AND THE UNIVERSE Reading 1: Alien Planet (Space Science) Reading 2: Life on other planets (Space Science)	Our journey into space	*Key reading skill*: Scanning to find information Previewing Understanding key vocabulary Reading for main ideas Working out meaning Scanning to predict content Making inferences	Vocabulary to describe giving evidence and supporting an argument (e.g. *studies, reports, research, an expert*)	

GRAMMAR	CRITICAL THINKING	WRITING
Collocations with *temperature* Describing a graph *Grammar for writing*: • Comparative and superlative adjectives	• Analyze a graph • Evaluate a table and a graph	*Academic writing skills*: • Introductory sentences for descriptive paragraphs about a graph *Writing task type*: Write sentences to describe a graph. *Writing task*: Describe a graph.
Prepositions of movement *Grammar for writing*: • Subject and verb agreement	• Analyze a diagram • Apply information to a description and a diagram	*Academic writing skills*: • Ordering events in a process • Eliminating irrelevancies *Writing task type*: Write a process paragraph. *Writing task*: Write a process paragraph to describe the Sydney triathlon.
Collocations with *business* Business vocabulary *Grammar for writing*: • Past and present tenses • Clauses with *when*	• Analyze a spider diagram • Create a timeline to organize events	*Academic writing skills*: • Adding detail *Writing task type*: Write a narrative paragraph. *Writing task*: Write a narrative paragraph about the business history of Google.
Noun phrases with *of* Adjectives to describe people *Grammar for writing*: • Subject and object pronouns • Possessive adjectives	• Apply information to a category • Analyze photographs • Create an idea wheel to categorize information	*Academic writing skills*: • Concluding sentences *Writing task type*: Write an explanatory paragraph. *Writing task*: Describe a person you admire and explain why.
Giving evidence and supporting an argument *should* and *it is important to* *Grammar for writing*: • Developing sentence structure • Infinitive of purpose	• Analyze an essay question • Evaluate arguments for and against • Create evidence and examples for arguments	*Academic writing skills*: • Essay organization *Writing task type*: Write a balanced opinion essay. *Writing task*: Exploring space is very expensive. Some people think that it is too expensive. However, other people think it is a good way for governments to spend our money. Discuss both points of view and give your opinion.

UNL**O**CK UNIT STRUCTURE

The units in *Unlock Reading & Writing Skills* are carefully scaffolded so that students are taken step-by-step through the writing process.

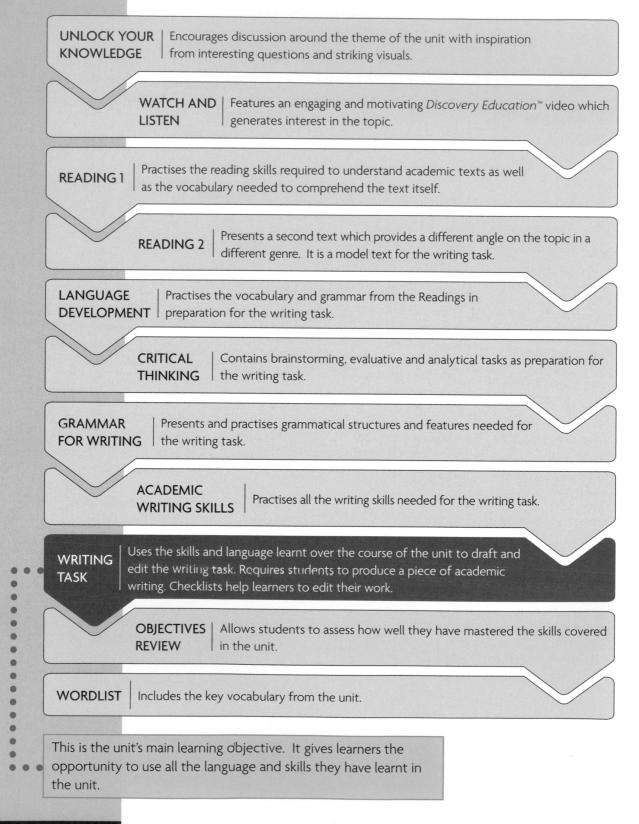

UNLOCK YOUR KNOWLEDGE	Encourages discussion around the theme of the unit with inspiration from interesting questions and striking visuals.
WATCH AND LISTEN	Features an engaging and motivating *Discovery Education™* video which generates interest in the topic.
READING 1	Practises the reading skills required to understand academic texts as well as the vocabulary needed to comprehend the text itself.
READING 2	Presents a second text which provides a different angle on the topic in a different genre. It is a model text for the writing task.
LANGUAGE DEVELOPMENT	Practises the vocabulary and grammar from the Readings in preparation for the writing task.
CRITICAL THINKING	Contains brainstorming, evaluative and analytical tasks as preparation for the writing task.
GRAMMAR FOR WRITING	Presents and practises grammatical structures and features needed for the writing task.
ACADEMIC WRITING SKILLS	Practises all the writing skills needed for the writing task.
WRITING TASK	Uses the skills and language learnt over the course of the unit to draft and edit the writing task. Requires students to produce a piece of academic writing. Checklists help learners to edit their work.
OBJECTIVES REVIEW	Allows students to assess how well they have mastered the skills covered in the unit.
WORDLIST	Includes the key vocabulary from the unit.

This is the unit's main learning objective. It gives learners the opportunity to use all the language and skills they have learnt in the unit.

UNL🔗CK MOTIVATION

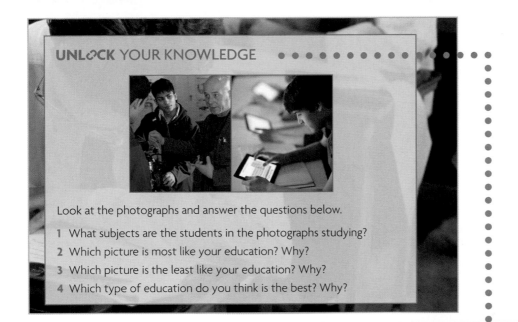

UNL🔗CK YOUR KNOWLEDGE

Look at the photographs and answer the questions below.

1 What subjects are the students in the photographs studying?
2 Which picture is most like your education? Why?
3 Which picture is the least like your education? Why?
4 Which type of education do you think is the best? Why?

PERSONALIZE

Unlock encourages students to bring their own knowledge, experiences and opinions to the topics. This motivates students to relate the topics to their own contexts.

DISCOVERY EDUCATION™ VIDEO

Thought-provoking videos from *Discovery Education*™ are included in every unit throughout the course to introduce topics, promote discussion and motivate learners. The videos provide a new angle on a wide range of academic subjects.

> ❝ The video was excellent! It helped with raising students' interest in the topic. It was well-structured and the language level was appropriate. ❞
>
> Maria Agata Szczerbik,
> United Arab Emirates University,
> Al-Ain, UAE

UNL😊CK CRITICAL THINKING

> " The Critical thinking sections present a difficult area in an engaging and accessible way.
> Shirley Norton, London School of English, UK "

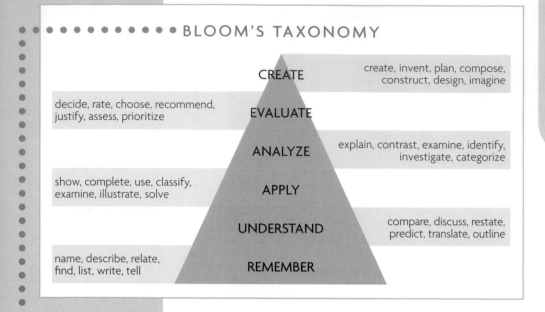

BLOOM'S TAXONOMY

CREATE — create, invent, plan, compose, construct, design, imagine

decide, rate, choose, recommend, justify, assess, prioritize — EVALUATE

ANALYZE — explain, contrast, examine, identify, investigate, categorize

show, complete, use, classify, examine, illustrate, solve — APPLY

UNDERSTAND — compare, discuss, restate, predict, translate, outline

name, describe, relate, find, list, write, tell — REMEMBER

BLOOM'S TAXONOMY

The Critical Thinking sections in *Unlock* are based on Benjamin Bloom's classification of learning objectives. This ensures learners develop their **lower-** and **higher-order thinking skills**, ranging from demonstrating **knowledge** and **understanding** to in-depth **evaluation**.
The margin headings in the Critical Thinking sections highlight the exercises which develop Bloom's concepts.

LEARN TO THINK

Learners engage in **evaluative** and **analytical tasks** that are designed to ensure they do all of the thinking and information-gathering required for the end-of-unit writing task.

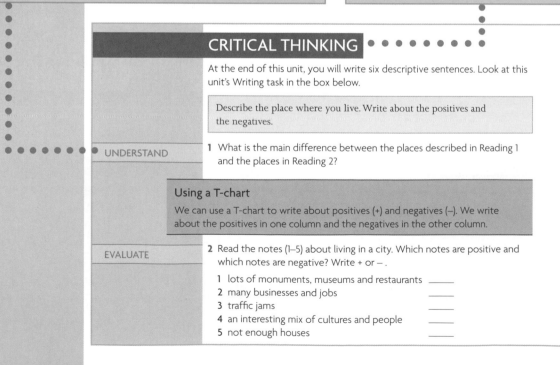

CRITICAL THINKING

At the end of this unit, you will write six descriptive sentences. Look at this unit's Writing task in the box below.

> Describe the place where you live. Write about the positives and the negatives.

UNDERSTAND

1 What is the main difference between the places described in Reading 1 and the places in Reading 2?

Using a T-chart
We can use a T-chart to write about positives (+) and negatives (–). We write about the positives in one column and the negatives in the other column.

EVALUATE

2 Read the notes (1–5) about living in a city. Which notes are positive and which notes are negative? Write + or – .

1 lots of monuments, museums and restaurants _____
2 many businesses and jobs _____
3 traffic jams _____
4 an interesting mix of cultures and people _____
5 not enough houses _____

UNLOCK RESEARCH

THE CAMBRIDGE LEARNER CORPUS ⊙

The **Cambridge Learner Corpus** is a bank of official Cambridge English exam papers. Our exclusive access means we can use the corpus to carry out unique research and identify the most common errors learners make. That information is used to ensure the *Unlock* syllabus teaches the most **relevant language**.

THE WORDS YOU NEED

Language Development sections provide vocabulary and grammar building tasks that are further practised in the **UNLOCK ONLINE** Workbook. The glossary and end-of-unit wordlists provide definitions, pronunciation and handy summaries of all the key vocabulary.

PLACES	UNIT 1

⊙ LANGUAGE DEVELOPMENT

NOUNS, VERBS AND ADJECTIVES

1 Look at the sentence below and the numbered words. Match words (1–3) to the word classes below.

> (1) Delhi (2) has many (3) beautiful (1) monuments, (3) interesting (1) museums and (3) modern (1) restaurants.

noun _____

verb _____

2

3

GRAMMAR FOR WRITING

EXPLANATION

Sentence structure 1: Subject + verb

A sentence has to have a subject and a verb. The subject of a sentence can be a noun or a noun phrase. A noun phrase is a group of words that acts like a noun. The verb can also be one word or a group of words.

subject (noun or noun phrase)	verb	
The people in the town	are	friendly.
The village	does not have	a shop.
My brother	lives	in the city.

ACADEMIC LANGUAGE

Unique research using the **Cambridge English Corpus** has been carried out into academic language, in order to provide learners with relevant, academic vocabulary from the start (CEFR A1 and above). This addresses a gap in current academic vocabulary mapping and ensures learners are presented with carefully selected words they will find essential during their studies.

GRAMMAR FOR WRITING

The grammar syllabus is carefully designed to help learners become good writers of English. There is a strong focus on sentence structure, word agreement and referencing, which are important for **coherent** and **organized** academic writing.

> " The language development is clear and the strong lexical focus is positive as learners feel they make more progress when they learn more vocabulary.
> Colleen Wackrow,
> Princess Nourah Bint Abdulrahman University, Al-Riyadh, Kingdom of Saudi Arabia "

UNLOCK SOLUTIONS

FLEXIBLE

Unlock is available in a range of print and digital components, so teachers can mix and match according to their requirements.

UNLOCK ONLINE WORKBOOKS

The **UNLOCK ONLINE** Workbooks are accessed via activation codes packaged with the Student's Books. These **easy-to-use** workbooks provide interactive exercises, games, tasks, and further practice of the language and skills from the Student's Books in the Cambridge LMS, an engaging and modern learning environment.

CAMBRIDGE LEARNING MANAGEMENT SYSTEM (LMS)

The Cambridge LMS provides teachers with the ability to track learner progress and save valuable time thanks to automated marking functionality. Blogs, forums and other tools are also available to facilitate communication between students and teachers.

UNLOCK EBOOKS

The *Unlock* Student's Books and Teacher's Books are also available as interactive eBooks. With answers and *Discovery Education™* videos embedded, the eBooks provide a great alternative to the printed materials.

COURSE COMPONENTS

- Each level of *Unlock* consists of two Student's Books: **Reading & Writing** and **Listening & Speaking** and an accompanying Teacher's Book for each. Online Workbooks are packaged with each Student's Book.
- Look out for the UNLOCK ONLINE symbols in the Student's Books which indicate that additional practice of that skill or language area is available in the Online Workbook.
- Every *Unlock* Student's Book is delivered both in print format and as an interactive **eBook for tablet devices**.
- The *Unlock* Teacher's Books contain additional writing tasks, tests, teaching tips and research projects for students.
- *Presentation Plus* **software for interactive whiteboards** is available for all Student's Books.

READING AND WRITING

Student's Book and Online Workbook Pack*	978-1-107-61399-7	978-1-107-61400-0	978-1-107-61526-7	978-1-107-61525-0
Teacher's Book with DVD*	978-1-107-61401-7	978-1-107-61403-1	978-1-107-61404-8	978-1-107-61409-3
Presentation Plus (interactive whiteboard software)	978-1-107-63800-6	978-1-107-65605-5	978-1-107-67624-4	978-1-107-68245-0

*eBook available from **www.cambridge.org/unlock**

LISTENING AND SPEAKING

Student's Book and Online Workbook Pack*	978-1-107-67810-1	978-1-107-68232-0	978-1-107-68728-8	978-1-107-63461-9
Teacher's Book with DVD*	978-1-107-66211-7	978-1-107-64280-5	978-1-107-68154-5	978-1-107-65052-7
Presentation Plus (interactive whiteboard software)	978-1-107-66424-1	978-1-107-69582-5	978-1-107-63543-2	978-1-107-64381-9

*eBook available from **www.cambridge.org/unlock**

The complete course audio is available from **www.cambridge.org/unlock**

LEARNING OBJECTIVES

Watch and listen	Watch and understand a video about places
Reading skills	Scan for numbers
Academic writing skills	Use capital letters and full stops correctly
Writing task	Write descriptive sentences

UNL**O**CK YOUR KNOWLEDGE

Look at the photograph and answer the questions below.

1 Where is the place in the photograph?
2 Is the city the same or different to the place where you live? How?
3 Would you like to live here? Why / Why not?

WATCH AND LISTEN

PREPARING TO WATCH

UNDERSTANDING
KEY VOCABULARY

1 Match the words (1–3) to their opposites (a–c). Use the glossary on page 194 to help you.

1 city   a rural
2 modern   b village
3 urban   c traditional

WHILE WATCHING

UNDERSTANDING
MAIN IDEAS

2 ▶ Watch the video. Circle the correct words to complete the sentences.

1 The Khanty village in Siberia is in *Russia / Egypt*.
2 The Khanty village is very *cold / hot*.
3 Siwa is in *Russia / Egypt*.
4 Siwa is a *village / town*.
5 Siwa is very *cold / hot*.

UNDERSTANDING
DETAIL

3 ▶ Watch again. Write true (T) or false (F) next to the statements below.

1 The Khanty village is in Moscow. _____
2 Temperatures in Siberia can reach -53°C. _____
3 People in the Khanty village travel on skis. _____
4 The Khanty village is very modern. _____
5 Siwa is in the Sahara desert. _____
6 Temperatures in the Sahara desert can reach 68°C. _____
7 Many people in Siwa use donkeys instead of cars. _____
8 There is a new road in Siwa. _____
9 People think that life in Siwa will change. _____

4 Look at the underlined word from the video. What do you think *remote* means?

> In the far north of Russia, thousands of miles from the capital Moscow, Siberia is one of the most <u>remote</u> places in the world.

  a far away from other places
  b close to other places

5 How did you find the answer to Exercise 4?
  1 from the photographs in the video
  2 from the other words in the sentence
  3 from the way the speaker talks

6 ▶ Watch the video. Listen for the words (1–3) below. Circle the words and phrases that have the same meaning.

  1 isolated (adj)   *not remote / remote*
  2 block (v)   *close a space / open a space*
  3 oasis (n)   *mountains in a desert /*
                          lakes or rivers in a desert

DISCUSSION

7 Work with a partner. Discuss the questions below.
  1 Where would you prefer to live: Siwa or Siberia? Why?
  2 In the video, it says that people in Siwa think that the new road will change their town. What changes do you think they will see? Think about the following:
     a language
     b jobs
     c transport

8 Look at your answers. Are the changes mainly good or bad?

PREPARING TO READ

UNDERSTANDING
KEY VOCABULARY

1 Match the words (1–4) to their definitions (a–d).

1 population
2 pollution
3 housing
4 traffic

a houses for people to live in
b the number of cars on a road
c when the air, water or earth is dirty and bad for people, plants and animals
d the number of people living in a place

MAKING
PREDICTIONS

2 Read the title of the article opposite. What do you think *mega* means?

a very busy
b very good
c very big

3 Read the article and check your answer.

WHILE READING

READING FOR
MAIN IDEAS

UNLOCK
ONLINE

4 Write true (T) or false (F) next to the statements below.

1 There are more megacities now than in 1950. _____
2 There are many opportunities to study in megacities. _____
3 Many people leave the countryside and move to a city. _____
4 Most megacities are in Europe. _____
5 Megacities can be very interesting places to live. _____
6 Many megacities have problems with housing. _____

READING FOR
DETAIL

5 Read the article again and write the words from the box in the correct place in the table below.

> mix of different people   interesting places to visit   lots of jobs
> traffic jams   good place to study   housing problem
> important industries   busy trains

Tokyo	
Delhi	
Cairo	

Rise of the
MEGACITIES

Megacity: a city with more than 10 million inhabitants

The number of megacities is growing very quickly. In the 1950s, there were only two megacities in the world.

Today, 4 percent of the world's urban population live in a megacity. Studies show that there will be 8 billion people in the world in 2025. Experts say that there will be 27 megacities.

Today, more than twenty cities in the world are megacities. 75% are in Asia, South America and Africa. More and more people around the world are leaving their homes in the countryside and moving to the city.

Many megacities have better opportunities, such as more jobs and a choice of schools and universities. Megacities are also exciting places to live – there are lots of different people, languages and restaurants and there are many interesting things to do.

However, megacities have problems, too. The cities are very big and this can cause problems like pollution or poor housing.

TOKYO, JAPAN
36.4 MILLION

Tokyo is an exciting, modern city in the east of Japan. There are lots of jobs because most big companies in Japan are in Tokyo. It is also an excellent place to study – 20% of Japan's universities are in the city. However, Tokyo is very busy and the traffic is very bad. More than 6.3 million people use the trains every day.

DELHI, INDIA
22.5 MILLION

Delhi is in the north of India. It has many beautiful monuments, interesting museums and modern restaurants. There is an exciting mix of different cultures in the city, and there are four official languages: Hindi, Urdu, Punjabi and English. However, there are not enough houses in some parts of Delhi. This means that many people live in large slums in the city.

CAIRO, EGYPT
16.9 MILLION

Cairo is the capital of Egypt and it is the largest city in Africa. Cairo has important car and film industries. The city is the centre of many government offices and has many universities, one of which is over 1,200 years old.

6 Find and circle all the numbers in the article (page 19).

7 Write a number from the article in each gap to complete the notes.

1 number of megacities in 1950 = _____
2 number of megacities in 2025 = _____
3 percent of people in the world that live in a megacity = _____ %
4 global population in 2025 = _____ billion
5 number of people who use the trains in Tokyo = _____ million
6 percent of Japanese universities in Tokyo = _____ %
7 number of people living in Delhi = _____ million
8 number of official languages spoken in Delhi = _____
9 age of Cairo's oldest university = _____ years old

Scanning for numbers

Scanning helps you find specific information or details in a text. We often scan a text for numbers to find important facts and figures about a topic.

READING BETWEEN THE LINES

8 Look at the word *slums* underlined in the article. What do you think it means?

a a very poor and crowded area in a city
b a very untidy house
c a very expensive area in the centre of a city

DISCUSSION

9 Work with a partner. Discuss the questions below.

1 Are there any megacities in or near your country?
2 What are the advantages and disadvantages of living in the city?
3 Why are modern cities growing so quickly?
4 What are the best solutions to the problems of pollution and poor housing?

READING 2

PREPARING TO READ

1 Read the title of the article on page 22. What general topic do you think the article is about?

a geography
b tourism
c history

2 Read the introduction and check your answer.

3 Circle the word or words in the introduction that tell you the answer.

WHILE READING

4 Match the headings (1–3) to the paragraphs in the article (a–c).

1 A big city
2 A mountain village
3 A house by the beach

5 Look at the summaries of the paragraphs. Cross out the incorrect words in bold and write the correct words. The first one has been done for you as an example.

1 The Atal family live in a ~~city~~ *village*. It is a **busy** place. The mountains are very **cold**.
2 Kate and Julian Foxton live in the **north** of England. The area is great for **theatres**. The houses are quite **cheap**.
3 Chafic and Aline Halwany live in a **small** city. People learn **English** and French in the town centre. There is quite a lot of traffic **at night**.

READING BETWEEN THE LINES

6 Work with a partner. Discuss your ideas about the questions below.

1 Why are homestays cheap places to stay?
2 How many languages do the Halwanys speak?
3 Do Kate and Julian have children?

DISCUSSION

7 Work with a partner. Discuss the questions below.

1 Why do people like to go to villages or the countryside on holiday?
2 What are the advantages and disadvantages of living in the countryside?
3 Why do young people leave the countryside to live in the city?

HOMESTAY HOLIDAYS:
a home away from home

Homestays are becoming more and more popular, and people around the world are offering their homes as hotels. Homestays offer cheap places to stay, and the chance for guests to see the area like a local. They are very popular with students who want to stay in another country and learn a language. We asked three families who run homestays to tell us about where they live.

a

The Atal family

Our family home is in the north of Nepal, in the Himalayan mountains, in the village of Manang. The village is quite small and very quiet. It is a very friendly place. The mountains are extremely beautiful. You can go for long walks and swim in the rivers but there are no shops, cinemas or cafés.

b

Kate and Julian Foxton

Our two-bed house is by the sea in the south-west of England. It is 15 minutes' drive to the nearest village of Portreath. There are lots of beaches, rivers and forests and it is very quiet. We spend a lot of time reading books, watching films and going for walks. Our area is great for sports like surfing, kayaking and mountain biking. However, the houses here are expensive, which can be a problem for local people. There are no buses or trains here, so it can be difficult to get around without a car.

c

Chafic and Aline Halwany

Our home is near the centre of Beirut, Lebanon, one of the largest cities in the Middle East. There are lots of cafés and restaurants, which open late at night. We love it here because it's so friendly and you can always find what you need – lots of people come to stay to learn Arabic and French. However, it can be noisy at night, and there is quite a lot of traffic during the day.

⊙ LANGUAGE DEVELOPMENT

NOUNS, VERBS AND ADJECTIVES

1 Look at the sentence below and the numbered words. Match words (1–3) to the word classes below.

> (1) Delhi (2) has many (3) beautiful (1) monuments, (3) interesting (1) museums and (3) modern (1) restaurants.

noun _____

verb _____

adjective _____

2 Match the sentence halves.

1 A noun is a word that   a describes a noun.
2 A verb is a word that   b refers to a place or thing.
3 An adjective is a word that   c describes an action.

3 Write the words from the box in the correct place in the table below.

> live   town   excellent   drive
> exciting   have   café   different   building

noun	verb	adjective

EXPLANATION

Adjectives

We use *adjectives* to describe nouns. We use the structure *adjective + noun*.

	adjective	+ noun
Beirut is an	interesting	city.
There are many	excellent	restaurants.

Adjectives are never plural.

a different place → ~~some differents places~~ → some different places

4 Match the adjectives (1–5) to their opposites (a–e).

1	interesting	**a**	expensive
2	cheap	**b**	boring
3	polluted	**c**	clean
4	beautiful	**d**	quiet
5	noisy	**e**	ugly

5 Write an adjective in each gap to complete the sentences.

1 There are lots of cars and traffic jams. The air is very _____ .
2 This is an _____ city. Everything costs a lot of money.
3 My village is very _____ . There isn't any noise.
4 London is a really _____ place. There are lots of things to do.
5 The building looks horrible. It's very _____ .

CRITICAL THINKING

At the end of this unit, you will write six descriptive sentences. Look at this unit's Writing task in the box below.

> Describe the place where you live. Write about the positives and the negatives.

UNDERSTAND

1 What is the main difference between the places described in Reading 1 and the places in Reading 2?

Using a T-chart

We can use a T-chart to write about positives (+) and negatives (–). We write about the positives in one column and the negatives in the other column.

EVALUATE

2 Read the notes (1–5) about living in a city. Which notes are positive and which notes are negative? Write + or – .

1 lots of monuments, museums and restaurants _____
2 many businesses and jobs _____
3 traffic jams _____
4 an interesting mix of cultures and people _____
5 not enough houses _____

3 Write the notes (1–5) in the correct place in the T-chart.

positive (+)	negative (–)

4 Think of two more negative things and two more positive things about living in a city. Write them in the correct place in the T-chart.

5 Think of positive and negative things about living in a village in the countryside. Write your notes in the correct place in the T-chart. The first one in each column has been done for you as an example.

positive (+)	negative (–)
beautiful	boring

6 Think about where you live. What are the positive and negative things about where you live? Think about the things in the list below.

- things to do
- jobs
- transport
- people
- houses

7 Write your notes in the correct place in the T-chart.

positive (+)	negative (–)

WRITING

GRAMMAR FOR WRITING

Sentence structure 1: Subject + verb

A sentence has to have a subject and a verb. The subject of a sentence can be a noun or a noun phrase. A noun phrase is a group of words that acts like a noun. The verb can also be one word or a group of words.

subject (noun or noun phrase)	verb	
The people in the town	are	friendly.
The village	does not have	a shop.
My brother	lives	in the city.

UNLOCK ONLINE

1 Underline the subject and circle the verb in the sentences below.

   1 Paris is a beautiful city.
   2 The town does not have a park.
   3 I live in a small town.
   4 Istanbul has many attractions.
   5 Many students live in the city.
   6 The village is not very exciting.
   7 The shops are excellent.
   8 The houses in the town are not very expensive.

2 Rewrite the sentences with the correct form of the verb *be*.

   1 I Saudi _____
   2 He an engineer _____
   3 The people nice _____
   4 We happy _____
   5 Jakarta beautiful _____
   6 It a small village _____

3 Look at your answers to Exercise 2. Write *S* next to the subject and *V* next to the verb in each sentence.

EXPLANATION

There is / There are

We use *there is / there are* to explain the general features of a place. In these sentences we do not have a subject.

There is a beach.
There are many cafés.

We use *there is* when we talk about one thing (singular) and *there are* when we talk about many things (plural).

	there is / there are	noun / noun phrase
singular	There is	a cinema.
	There is not	a theatre.
plural	There are	lots of shops.
	There are not	many beaches.

4 Circle the correct word to complete the sentences.

1 There *is / are* many traffic jams in my town.
2 There *is / are* an excellent museum.
3 There *is / are* people from many different countries.
4 There *is / are* lots of flats in the city centre.
5 There *is / are* a beach and a river.
6 There *is / are* lots of jobs.

5 The sentences below are incorrect. Rewrite them with *there is / there are* to make them correct.

1 Five restaurants are in my town.

_____

2 A museum is in my town.

_____

3 A river is near my village.

_____

4 Lots of cars are in my city.

_____

6 Look at the fact file about the city of Doha. Write one sentence for each bullet point about Doha using *there is / there are*. The first one has been done for you as an example.

FACT FILE DOHA, QATAR

- many sports stadiums
- lots of museums
- twelve universities
- a port
- one airport
- many five-star hotels
- a castle

1 There are many sports stadiums.
2 _____
3 _____
4 _____
5 _____
6 _____
7 _____

ACADEMIC WRITING SKILLS

EXPLANATION

Capital letters and full stops

We use a *capital letter* at the beginning of a sentence. We use a *full stop* (.) at the end of a sentence.

He lives in Abu Dhabi.

We also use a capital letter with a *proper noun*.

france ➜ France
istanbul ➜ Istanbul
july ➜ July
saturday ➜ Saturday

We always use a capital letter for *I*.

I live in London.

7 Work with a partner. Put capital letters and full stops in the paragraph.

> I
> ꭗlive in a city called tarragona it is in spain it is a beautiful city there
> are many shops and restaurants the people are friendly there is a flower
> festival in june

WRITING TASK

> Describe the place where you live. Write about the positives and
> the negatives.

1 Look at the T-chart you made in the Critical thinking section (page 25). Choose three positive (+) things and three negative (–) things that you are going to write about.

2 Look at the paragraph planner below. Write three sentences describing positive things about where you live and three sentences describing negative things about where you live.

positive 1	
positive 2	
positive 3	
negative 1	
negative 2	
negative 3	

UNLOCK ONLINE

PLAN

WRITE A
FIRST DRAFT

3 Use the task checklist to review your sentences for content and structure.

TASK CHECKLIST	✔
Have you written about the place where you live?	
Have you written six sentences?	
Are there three positive sentences?	
Are there three negative sentences?	

4 Make any necessary changes to your sentences.

5 Now use the language checklist to edit your sentences for language errors which are common to A2 learners.

LANGUAGE CHECKLIST	✔
Have you used nouns, verbs and adjectives correctly?	
Does every sentence have a subject and a verb?	
Is the correct form of *there is / there are* used?	
Is *there is / there are* used to talk about general features?	
Have you used capital letters and full stops correctly?	

6 Make any necessary changes to your sentences.

OBJECTIVES REVIEW

7 Check your objectives.

I can ...

watch and understand a
video about places.

very
well

not very
well

scan for numbers.

very
well

not very
well

use capital letters and
full stops correctly.

very
well

not very
well

write descriptive
sentences.

very
well

not very
well

WORDLIST

UNIT VOCABULARY	
adjective (n)	boring (adj)
city (n)	cheap (adj)
countryside (n)	expensive (adj)
noun (n)	interesting (adj)
pollution (n)	modern (adj)
population (n)	noisy (adj)
traffic (n)	rural (adj)
verb (n)	traditional (adj)
beautiful (adj)	urban (adj)

LEARNING OBJECTIVES

Watch and listen	Watch and understand a video about a festival
Reading skills	Preview a text
Academic writing skills	Organize sentences into a paragraph
Writing task	Write a descriptive paragraph

FESTIVALS AND CELEBRATIONS UNIT 2

Sydney

UNLOCK YOUR KNOWLEDGE

Work with a partner. Look at the photographs and discuss the questions below.

1 What is happening in the photographs?
2 What countries do you think the photographs are from?

WATCH AND LISTEN

PREPARING TO WATCH

UNDERSTANDING
KEY VOCABULARY

1 Match the words and phrases (1–8) to their definitions (a–h).

1	a race	a	stories from a place or culture
2	folk stories	b	the way someone lives
3	a way of life	c	a competition to find the fastest person
4	take part	d	do an activity or sport
5	ancient	e	something that is in the culture of a group of people for a long time
6	a tradition		
7	unique	f	existed for a very, very long time
8	a jockey	g	a person who rides a horse in a competition
		h	very special or different to other things

USING YOUR
KNOWLEDGE

2 You are going to watch a video about a festival in Mongolia. Write true (T) or false (F) next to the statements below.

1 There are no Mongolian people living in northern China. _____

2 Mongolian people love horses. _____

3 Children can ride horses. _____

4 Horse riding is not a dangerous sport. _____

3 ▶ Watch the video and check your answers.

WHILE WATCHING

UNDERSTANDING
MAIN IDEAS

4 ▶ Watch again. Number the ideas (a–f) in the order you hear them.

a There are many horses in the race. _____

b It is not easy to ride the horses. _____

c The people prepare dinner and sing. _____

d The jockeys are all very young. _____

e The different groups of people each have their own culture. _____

f The Mongolians have a big summer festival. _____

5 ▶ Watch again. Circle the correct words to complete the sentences.

1 The region of Inner Mongolia has mountains and *lakes / grasslands*.
2 The Mongolians have a very *old / new* culture.
3 The festival is part of *Mongolian / Chinese* tradition.
4 'Naadam' is a type of *festival / game*.
5 About a *thousand / hundred* horses take part in the race.
6 The horses can run the long race because *they / the jockeys* are not big.
7 The jockeys *practise / run* for a long time before the race.
8 *The horses are / This horse race is* very old.

6 What do you think *horses are at the heart of Mongolian culture* means? Choose the best definition below.

1 Horses make Mongolians feel very happy.
2 Horses are a very important part of Mongolian culture.

7 The video says that the jockeys *show great skill*. Why is this? Choose the best two explanations below.

1 because this is the largest horse race in the world
2 because they are very young and small
3 because they do not have seats and they have nothing to hold with their feet

DISCUSSION

8 Work with a partner. Discuss the questions below.

1 How old do you think your culture is? Is it ancient, old or new?
2 What festivals are parts of your country's traditions?
3 Is it important to follow traditions and a way of life?
4 What do you think is at the heart of your culture?

READING 1

PREPARING TO READ

1 Match the words (1–3) to their definitions (a–c).

1 a sweet
2 a gift / a present
3 a stick

a a long, thin piece of wood
b a small piece of food, often made of sugar or chocolate
c something that you give to someone, usually on a special day

2 Write the words from the box in the gaps.

> hang   the ground   lucky   culture   a business   successful
> a company   celebrate   traditional

1 Something that is _____ follows a way of behaving that has continued for a long time.
2 _____ is the surface of the Earth.
3 If you _____ something, you put it somewhere high so part of it falls down.
4 _____ or _____ is an organization that sells goods or services.
5 _____ is the habits, traditions and beliefs of a country or group of people.
6 Many people believe that _____ objects make good things happen to you.
7 If you _____ , you have a party or a meal because it is a special day or because something good has happened.
8 Something that is _____ has a good result.

3 Look at the photographs, titles and subtitles in the article opposite. Choose and circle the topic of the article (a–c).

a celebrations around the world
b weddings around the world
c birthdays around the world

Previewing

Before you read, look at the photographs, title and subtitles. This gives you a lot of information about the topic of the text before you read. It will help you understand the text better when you read it.

4 Read the article and check your answer.

Celebrate!

Piñatas

In Mexico, children often have piñatas on their birthday. The child's parents put chocolates and other sweets inside the piñata and hang it on a tree. Then the children hit the piñata with a stick. It breaks and the sweets fall out on to the ground.

Noodles

In China, people celebrate weddings with an eight-course meal, because the word *eight* sounds like the word for *good luck*. The last dish of the meal is always noodles. The noodles are long and thin. You have to eat them in one piece – you can't cut them. In Chinese culture, long noodles are lucky. Long noodles mean you will have a long life.

Business birthdays

A business birthday shows that a company is successful. Many businesses in the USA celebrate important birthdays, like 10, 50 or 150 years. Companies hold parties and send cards. Companies sometimes make TV adverts. It is a good opportunity to advertise the business.

Name days

As well as a birthday, many people in Southern Europe also celebrate their name day. In Greece, name days are more important than birthdays. People have big parties and open their houses to anybody who wants to come. People bring small gifts, often flowers or a box of sweets.

Islamic New Year

In the UAE and other Muslim countries across the world, people celebrate Eid. *Eid* means *festival* or *celebration*. During Eid, people visit family and friends, as well as people who are sick or in hospital. They give presents, such as sweets and food. Children receive toys, too. Children often wear special traditional clothes during the Eid celebrations.

READING FOR
MAIN IDEAS

UNL🔗CK
ONLINE

READING FOR
DETAIL

RECOGNIZING
TEXT TYPE

WHILE READING

5 Read the article again. Match the celebrations (1–5) to the countries (a–e).

1 piñata
2 noodles
3 name day
4 sweets and food
5 business birthday

a China
b Mexico
c the UAE
d Greece
e the USA

6 Read the article again and write true (T) or false (F) next to the statements below.

1 Piñatas have flowers inside them.   _____
2 Long noodles are unlucky in Chinese culture.   _____
3 Many companies in the USA celebrate business birthdays. _____
4 On a name day, people bring gifts.   _____
5 During Eid, children wear special clothes.   _____

READING BETWEEN THE LINES

7 Where would you find this article?

a in a newspaper
b in an academic journal

8 Circle the features that helped you find the answer.

> photographs   colour of text   length of paragraphs
> title   number of paragraphs   layout of article

DISCUSSION

9 Work with a partner. Discuss the questions below.

1 What birthdays and special days do you celebrate?
2 What do you do on these days?
3 What is your favourite celebration? Why?

READING 2

PREPARING TO READ

1 Look at the words and circle the correct definition.

1 activities
  a things people do
  b buildings
2 history
  a something happening now
  b something that happened in
    the past

3 popular
  a something many people enjoy
  b very difficult
4 highlights
  a places
  b the most important parts

2 Read paragraph A in the text below and circle the proper nouns.

Proper nouns are names of people, countries, cities, festivals and nationalities. Days of the week and months are also proper nouns.

Muscat Festival

A One of the most important festivals in Oman is the Muscat Festival. The festival lasts for about one month and takes place in February every year. During the festival, many activities are available for people to take part in.

B Large numbers of people, including Omanis and visitors to Oman, go to the different events. The events are a celebration of both Omani and international history and traditions. The events take place in different places across the country. Many businesses show their products for people to look at and buy.

C The Muscat Festival also includes the very popular six-day Tour of Oman cycling race. Professional cyclists from around the world take part in the race. The race is nearly 1,000 kilometres long, and it takes the cyclists up the beautiful Jabal Al Akhdhar – the Green Mountain.

D Other highlights of the Muscat Festival include the chance to try out different types of food at the Oman Food Festival. The Muscat Art Festival also offers visitors Arabic music, concerts and plays, and other entertainment for the whole family. The Festival of Lights is one of the most popular events at the Muscat Festival.

E The Muscat Festival is very international, with people visiting from countries as far away as Brazil and Cuba. Visitors also arrive from Italy, India, Russia, South Korea, Spain, Tunisia and Turkey, as well as many other countries. They enjoy the amazing clothes, food and music. Some people just enjoy the mix of different cultures.

3 Answer the questions below.

   1 What country is the Muscat Festival in? _____

   2 When is the Muscat Festival? _____

4 Read paragraph A on page 39 again and check your answers.

WHILE READING

5 Read the text on page 39. Match the ideas (1–5) to the paragraphs (A–E).

   1 the countries people visit from
   2 how long the Muscat Festival lasts
   3 different events in the Festival
   4 international culture
   5 the Tour of Oman

6 Read the text again. Put words in the gaps to complete the sentences.

   1 The Muscat Festival happens in the month of _____ .
   2 People from all over the world _____ the festival.
   3 The English name for the Jabal Al Akhdhar is _____ .
   4 You can see plays at the _____ .
   5 The Festival of Lights is a very _____ event.
   6 Visitors enjoy clothes, _____ and _____ .

READING BETWEEN THE LINES

7 Where would you find this text?

   a in a textbook on Oman culture
   b in a textbook on the Oman economy

8 What other topics would you expect to find in the book?
Add two more to the list.

   1 _food_   3 _____
   2 _theatre_   4 _____

DISCUSSION

9 Work with a partner. Discuss the questions below.

   1 Would you like to visit Oman?
   2 What information about festivals would you give a visitor to your
      country? Answer the questions below.
      a What is the festival?   **c** Where is it?
      b When is it?   **d** What happens?

READING FOR
MAIN IDEAS

UNLOCK
ONLINE

READING FOR
DETAIL

RECOGNIZING
TEXT TYPE

⊙ LANGUAGE DEVELOPMENT

EXPLANATION

Prepositions of time and place: *on, in, at*

ON: We use *on* with a date or a day.

My birthday is **on** 1st May / **on** Saturday.

IN: We use *in* with a month and with *the morning, the afternoon* and *the evening.*
We also use *in* with a country or town.

My birthday is **in** May.
We eat dinner **in** the morning.
We celebrate New Year **in** France / **in** Paris.

AT: We use *at* with a time or with *night* and *the weekend.*
We also use *at* with *school, college, university, work* and *home.*

We eat dinner **at** 5 o'clock **at** night.
We have a party **at** school.

1 Write the words from the box in the correct place in the table below.

UNL⊘CK
ONLINE

> school   college   June   Sunday   home   work   a town   Istanbul
> the evening   the morning   night   1ˢᵗ January   my country
> Syria   8 o'clock   Tuesday

	on	*in*	*at*
places			
times			

2 Write *on, in* or *at* in the gaps to complete the sentences.

1 People have parties _____ work with their colleagues.
2 We have a meal _____ Saturday.
3 The festival is _____ November.
4 My brother's wedding is _____ 2nd December.
5 The children wake up _____ 7 o'clock.
6 People celebrate New Year _____ Australia.
7 We stay _____ home for the whole day.
8 We eat dinner late _____ night.

ADVERBS OF FREQUENCY

We use adverbs of frequency to talk about habits. They tell us how often someone does something. Adverbs of frequency go before the verb in a sentence.

3 Read the sentences (1–3) from Reading 1 and underline the adverbs of frequency.

   1 In Mexico, children often have piñatas on their birthday.
   2 In China, people always celebrate weddings with an eight-course meal.
   3 Companies sometimes make TV adverts.

4 Write the adverbs from the box in the gaps on the timeline.

usually   always   sometimes

never ➔ (1) _____ ➔ often ➔ (2) _____ ➔ (3) _____

5 Write the adverbs from the timeline in the gaps to make sentences that are true for you.

   1 I _____ visit my parents in the holidays.
   2 I _____ give my friends a present on their birthday.
   3 I _____ celebrate New Year.
   4 I _____ go to weddings.
   5 I _____ eat sweets on special occasions.

6 Work with a partner. Compare and discuss your answers.

CRITICAL THINKING

At the end of this unit, you will write a descriptive paragraph. Look at this unit's Writing task in the box below.

> Describe a festival or special event.

APPLY

1 Look at the calendar opposite. You are going to fill it in with this year's important events.

   1 Work with a partner. Write the names of four festivals from your country on the calendar.
   2 Write any personal or family celebrations on the calendar (for example, weddings, birthdays, graduation days, etc.).

January	February	March	April

May	June	July	August

September	October	November	December

2 Look at the events on the calendar. Which events do you think would be interesting to people from another country? Why?

I think our national day would be interesting because ...

Using a spider diagram to organize ideas

Before you write, you need to decide what to write about. A spider diagram can help you organize your ideas.

CREATE

3 Choose one event on your calendar.

1 Write the name of the event in the centre of the diagram.
2 Write about the topics below in the correct part of the spider diagram.
   - when the event is
   - where the event is
   - what people eat and drink at the event
   - what people do at the event
   - what people wear at the event

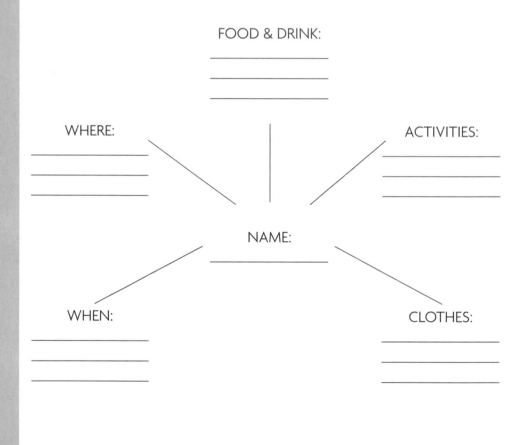

FOOD & DRINK:
_____
_____
_____

WHERE:
_____
_____
_____

ACTIVITIES:
_____
_____
_____

NAME:
_____

WHEN:
_____
_____
_____

CLOTHES:
_____
_____
_____

WRITING

GRAMMAR FOR WRITING

EXPLANATION

Sentence structure 2: subject and verb order

A sentence needs to have a *subject* and a *verb*. The verb comes after the subject. After the verb, we can have a *noun* (usually called an *object*), an *adjective* or a *prepositional phrase*.

subject	verb	noun phrase
I	visit	my family.

subject	verb	adjective
The people	are	happy.

subject	verb	prepositional phrase
The festival	is	in May.

UNLOCK ONLINE

1 In each sentence (1–5), underline the subject and circle the verb.

1 The children wear traditional clothes.
2 My family and I watch the fireworks.
3 I visit my aunt and uncle.
4 People in the UK celebrate university graduation.
5 My parents and I go to the town centre.

2 In each sentence (1–5), underline the part of the sentence that comes after the verb. Then write *N* for noun, *A* for adjective and *P* for prepositional phrase.

1 My family eat at home. _____
2 The costumes are beautiful. _____
3 We exchange presents. _____
4 I celebrate in the evening. _____
5 The festival is traditional. _____

3 Put the words in order to make sentences.

1 celebrate / People in Scotland / New Year /.

_____

2 on Sunday / My parents and I / cook /.

_____

3 excited / are / The men in my town /.

_____

4 eat / All my family / in the morning /.

_____

5 do not visit / my grandparents / We /.

_____

Prepositional phrases

Sometimes a sentence can have an object and a prepositional phrase.
The prepositional phrase comes after the object.

noun phrase (subject)	verb phrase	noun phrase (object)	prepositional phrase
People in Mexico	eat	a special meal	in the evening.

We can also put the prepositional phrase at the beginning of the sentence,
followed by a comma.

prepositional phrase	noun phrase (subject)	verb phrase	noun phrase (object)
In the evening,	people in Mexico	eat	a special meal.

4 In each sentence (1–5), underline the prepositional phrase.

1 We watch concerts at night.
2 In India, people celebrate the Magh Bihu festival.
3 People clean their homes in the morning.
4 Children have parties at school.
5 On Saturday, we watch the parades.

ACADEMIC WRITING SKILLS

Paragraph organization 1: organizing sentences into a paragraph

In formal English, we put the sentences we write into paragraphs. A paragraph
is a group of sentences about the same topic. When we start to write about a
different topic, we start a new paragraph.

Look at the sentences below. They are from two different paragraphs.
Paragraph 1 is about a city. Paragraph 2 is about a festival.

Sort the sentences into two paragraphs. Write 1 or 2 next to each sentence.

Popfest is a music festival in the UK.   2

It is a very noisy city.   1

People wear waterproof shoes and coats. _____

In the summer, it is very hot. _____
It happens in July. _____
I live in Taipei. _____
There are lots of shops and restaurants. _____
People listen to music and dance. _____
It's a great place to live. _____

WRITING TASK

Describe a festival or special event.

UNLOCK ONLINE

PLAN

1 Look at the notes about a festival in the spider diagram. Use the information in the diagram to write words in the gaps in the paragraph below.

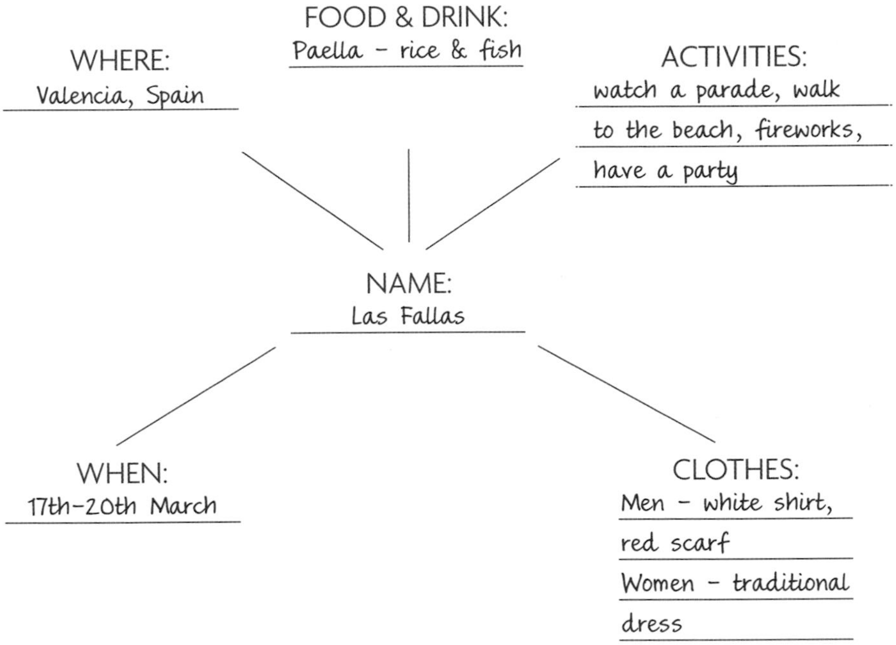

FOOD & DRINK:
Paella – rice & fish

WHERE:
Valencia, Spain

ACTIVITIES:
watch a parade, walk
to the beach, fireworks,
have a party

NAME:
Las Fallas

WHEN:
17th–20th March

CLOTHES:
Men – white shirt,
red scarf
Women – traditional
dress

In Valencia, Spain, people celebrate Las Fallas. Las Fallas is in
(1)_____ . It starts on the (2)_____ and
finishes on the 20th.
People watch a (3)_____ in the streets. In the evening,
everyone walks to the (4)_____ and has a party. There
are fireworks.
People also eat (5)_____ . It is a meal of
(6)_____ and fish. Men wear a white shirt and
a (7)_____ scarf and women wear traditional
(8)_____ .

2 Look at the spider diagram you completed in the Critical thinking section (page 44). Use your notes to write sentences in the paragraph planner about the event.

name and where	Thanksgiving is a festival in the USA.
when	
activities	
food and drink	
clothes	

3 Use the sentences in the paragraph planner to write a paragraph. Add *and* to join sentences.

4 Use the task checklist to review your paragraph for content and structure.

TASK CHECKLIST	✔
Are the sentences organized in a paragraph?	
Does the paragraph start with a sentence saying the name of the event and where people celebrate it?	
Does the paragraph say when the event is?	
Does the paragraph have information about the activities, food and drink, and clothes?	

5 Make any necessary changes to your paragraph.

6 Now use the language checklist to edit your paragraph for language errors which are common to A2 learners.

LANGUAGE CHECKLIST	✔
Have you used *on, in* and *at* correctly?	
Have you used adverbs of frequency correctly?	
Have you used correct sentence structure?	
Have you used prepositional phrases correctly?	

7 Make any necessary changes to your paragraph.

OBJECTIVES REVIEW

8 Check your objectives.

I can ...

watch and understand
a video about a festival

very
well

not very
well

preview a text.

very
well

not very
well

organize sentences into
a paragraph.

very
well

not very
well

write a descriptive
paragraph.

very
well

not very
well

WORDLIST

UNIT VOCABULARY			
business (n)	gift (n)	relative (n)	ancient (adj)
celebration (n)	ground (n)	stick (n)	lucky (adj)
company (n)	history (n)	celebrate (v)	popular (adj)
culture (n)	jockey (n)	hang (v)	successful (adj)
evening (n)	present (n)	take part (v)	traditional (adj)

LEARNING OBJECTIVES

Watch and Listen	Watch and understand a video about education and learning
Reading skills	Skim a text
Academic writing skills	Write a paragraph with a topic sentence, supporting sentences and a concluding sentence
Writing task	Write a descriptive paragraph

UNL◐CK YOUR KNOWLEDGE

Look at the photographs and answer the questions below.

1 What subjects are the students in the photographs studying?
2 Which picture is most like your education? Why?
3 Which picture is the least like your education? Why?
4 Which type of education do you think is the best? Why?

WATCH AND LISTEN

PREPARING TO WATCH

1 Write a word from the box in the gaps to complete the sentences below.

> class   lesson   train   choose   independent
> support   connection

1 There are a lot of international students in the __class__ this year.
2 If you want to be good at a sport, then you have to _____
   every day.
3 It's difficult to _____ which language to learn. English is useful, but
   Chinese and Spanish are also very popular.
4 We have an English _____ every morning.
5 It is important for children to be _____ . They should learn to think
   without a teacher telling them everything.
6 There is an important _____ between your education and your
   future job. If you have a good education, you will have a better job and
   make more money.
7 Parents should give _____ to their children and help with homework
   and studying.

2 Are the sentences in Exercise 1 true or false for you? Compare your
answers with a partner.

3 Work in pairs. You are going to watch a video about a lesson at a school
in the USA. Before you watch, look at the notes below. What type of
lesson do you think the video is about? _____

> • teacher   • choosing books   • love reading
> • children   • make notes

4 ▶ Watch the video and check your answers.

WHILE WATCHING

5 ▶ Watch again. Number the ideas (a–f) in the order you hear them.

UNDERSTANDING MAIN IDEAS

a The students discuss the books they read and their ideas. _____

b The teacher sits with the students and give support. _____

c The children choose a book to read. _____

d The students make a connection between the books and their own lives. _____

e The teacher reads a story to the class. _____

f The students make notes about the book. _____

6 ▶ Watch again. Match the sentence halves.

UNDERSTANDING DETAIL

1 The teacher wants children to find a book

2 Books about families, holidays and friends are good, because

3 The children find things in the books

4 The teacher does not

5 After the children read, the teacher

6 The teacher wants the children to

7 The teacher thinks that children make

a the children already know about these things.

b talks with them about their notes.

c that they can enjoy.

d understand the people in the books.

e which are like things in their own lives.

f a connection between stories and their own lives.

g help the children when they are reading their books.

7 The video says that *putting yourself in the character's shoes ... can help you understand the text*. What does this mean? Circle the best definition.

MAKING INFERENCES

a describe what a character in the story is wearing

b imagine you are in the same situation as a character in the story

c visit the same places as the character in the story

8 The teacher in the video says that *independent reading* is useful. What does she mean? Compare your answer with a partner. _____

DISCUSSION

9 Work with a partner. Discuss the questions below.

1 Do you think it is important for children to read books? Why / Why not?

2 What type of stories did you enjoy reading when you were a child?

3 Do you think children today read more or less than fifty years ago?

PREPARING TO READ

UNDERSTANDING KEY VOCABULARY

1 Match the words (1–12) to their definitions (a–l).

1	train	a	an amount of money given to a person by an organization to pay for their education
2	create		
3	return	b	officially ask for something
4	similar	c	be important
5	believe	d	go to a place where you were before
6	join	e	take care of (someone or something)
7	apply	f	learn the skills you need to do a job
8	look after	g	nearly the same as something else
9	local	h	become a member of an organization
10	professional	i	in an area near you
11	a scholarship	j	related to a job that needs special training or education
12	matter	k	think that something is true
		l	make something happen or exist

USING VISUALS TO PREDICT CONTENT

2 Look at the photograph in the article opposite and answer the questions.

1 What does the photograph show? _____
2 Who are the people in the photograph? _____
3 What year do you think the photograph was taken? _____

WHILE READING

SKIMMING

UNLOCK ONLINE

3 Read the article opposite quickly. You do not have to read every word. What is the article about?

a the FC Barcelona football stadium
b the UEFA Champions League
c the education of FC Barcelona football players

Skimming

When we skim a text, we read it quickly to find out the general topic of the text. Skimming can help you decide if a text is useful. You can then decide whether to read the text again properly.

4 Read the article and check your answers.

READING FOR MAIN IDEAS

5 Circle the statement that is the best summary of each paragraph.

1 Paragraph A
  a FC Barcelona has a very good training academy.
  b FC Barcelona is a very good football club.

LA MASIA: CREATING THE BEST FOOTBALLERS IN THE WORLD

A FC Barcelona's football academy, La Masia, trains some of the best footballers in Europe. Pep Guardiola, Lionel Messi, Cesc Fabregas and Gerard Pique are all graduates of La Masia. Many people believe that Barcelona is the best football team in Europe because of the training programme at the school. Now, FC Barcelona has opened similar academies all around the world, including in Egypt, Japan, America and Dubai.

B It is difficult to join the Barcelona academy. Every year, over 1,000 students apply, but only 70 students can live and study at the school. They are aged between 11 and 18. Seventy coaches, teachers, doctors, cooks, sports doctors and other staff look after the students. The academy costs about £5 million a year to run. But the students all have scholarships, so they don't pay any money. FC Barcelona pays for everything: the students' rooms, teachers, books and food.

C However, the students don't only learn football. FC Barcelona also wants to give their students a good academic education. It is important to the club that their students can still get good jobs if they don't become professional footballers. Students travel by bus to local schools each morning for four hours of study. The footballers return to La Masia after lunch and do football training in the afternoons.

D But is the students' academic education good enough? All the football training must make the students very tired and they spend less time at school than other children. That doesn't matter if you are one of the students who is good enough to become a professional footballer. But what happens to all the children who don't make it onto the team? La Masia produces excellent football players, but it is important to ask what happens to all the other children who train there.

2 Paragraph B
   a what students do at La Masia
   b what teachers and staff do at La Masia

3 Paragraph C
  a The students only learn about football.
  b The students also receive an academic education.
4 Paragraph D
  a Is the academic education at La Masia good enough?
  b Are the footballers at La Masia good enough?

READING FOR
DETAIL

6 Read the article again and write true (T), false (F) or does not say (DNS) next to the statements below.

1 Pep Guardiola, Lionel Messi, Cesc Fabregas and Gerard Pique all
  play for FC Barcelona.   _____
2 FC Barcelona has only one training academy.   _____
3 Every year, 75 students apply to go to the school.   _____
4 The students do not have to pay for their education.   _____
5 The food at La Masia is excellent.   _____
6 FC Barcelona wants to give students a good academic education. _____
7 The students walk to local schools in the morning.   _____
8 The students practise football at La Masia in the mornings.   _____

UNDERSTANDING
DISCOURSE

7 Look at the underlined words in the text. What do they mean – the football club or the training academy? Write the words in the correct place in the table below.

Barcelona football club	La Masia

READING BETWEEN THE LINES

MAKING
INFERENCES

8 Do all La Masia students become professional footballers?

9 Underline the sentences or parts of the article that tell you the answer.

DISCUSSION

10 Work with a partner. Discuss the questions below.

  1 What are the advantages and disadvantages of doing sport at school?
  2 Do you agree that professional football players should be paid more
    than doctors and teachers?

READING 2

PREPARING TO READ

1 Match the words to their definitions (1–10).

> a course   work experience   a lecture   exchange   notes
> a skill   a degree   a subject   a project   a schedule

1 words that you write down to help you remember something _____

2 a qualification given for completing a course of study at a university _____

3 an ability to do an activity well _____

4 a period of time in which a student works somewhere to learn about a job _____

5 give something to someone and get something similar from them _____

6 an area of knowledge studied at school or university _____

7 a plan that tells you when things will happen _____

8 a formal talk on a subject _____

9 a study of a particular subject done over a period of time _____

10 a set of lessons about a particular subject _____

2 You are going to read a text. Before you read, look quickly at the photographs, titles and the text on page 58. Where do you think you would see the text?

a on a university website

b on a secondary school website

3 What do you think the aim of the text is?

a to argue that people shouldn't go to Princeford University

b to argue that people should go to Princeford University

4 Read the text on page 58 and check your answers.

WHILE READING

5 Read the text again and answer the questions below.

1 What subject does Jessie study? _____

2 What subject does Serhan study? _____

3 What subject does Noor study? _____

Princeford University

Search 🔍

Contact us | A-Z

About the University | Study at Princeford | Students | Staff | My Princeford Experience

My Princeford Experience

At Princeford University, we know that every student is different. We have thousands of courses so everyone can find their perfect way to study. Here, three students tell us about what they study.

Jessie, 29, Practical Business

'I study a course called Practical Business. I have a very busy schedule. In the mornings, I study at university and in the afternoons, I do work experience in an office. I study Monday to Friday, five days a week. I have lectures and I study in the library with my friends. We talk about the course and exchange notes. It's really interesting. In the office, I learn a lot of practical skills. I like working with other people and I'm learning a lot. I study Practical Business because I'd like to have my own company. This course gives me all the practical skills to make my future company a success.'

Serhan, 23, Art History

'I study Art History online. I live in Turkey. I did my first degree at a Turkish university and I wanted to do my second degree at an English-speaking university. Studying online means I can study in English and live near my family and friends. I watch lectures online and download articles and notes. I can also talk to my lecturers online. I don't have to go to lectures, so I can study whenever I want. Art History is a really interesting subject. I don't know if I'll get a job in Art History – I just enjoy studying it for now.'

Noor, 18, Engineering

'I'm an international student from Malaysia. I study Engineering. In the mornings, we have big lectures, with all 250 students from the course. Three times a week, we have practical classes in the engineering labs. The classes are small and we work in small groups on our own projects. I also go to English lessons in the evening. In my subject, it is important to speak English well. The university has a very good programme for international students, and everybody is very helpful. I study Engineering because it's useful and I want to work all over the world.'

Contact us for more information.

Telephone: +61 3 2507 5492

Email: enquiries@princeford.edu.au

6 Match the sentence halves.

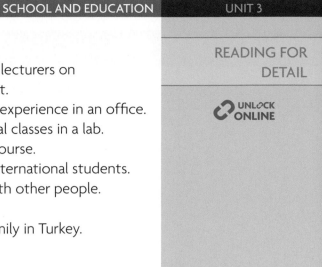

1 Jessie goes to lectures and   a talks to his lecturers on the internet.
2 Jessie likes
3 Serhan studies   b does work experience in an office.
4 Serhan lives   c has practical classes in a lab.
5 Serhan watches lectures and   d an online course.
6 Noor is from   e good for international students.
7 Noor has lectures and   f working with other people.
8 Noor thinks the university is   g Malaysia.
   h near his family in Turkey.

READING BETWEEN THE LINES

7 Why do Jessie, Serhan and Noor study their subjects? Tick the boxes to show their reasons.

	Jessie	Serhan	Noor
1 'I want to get a good job.'			
2 'I like studying.'			
3 'I want to learn practical skills.'			
4 'I want to work in different countries.'			
5 'I want to have my own business.'			

DISCUSSION

8 How useful do you think it is to study the following subjects? Put them in order from 1 (very useful) to 8 (not at all useful).

Medicine   _____
Mechanics   _____
Art   _____
Business   _____
History   _____
Cooking   _____
Foreign languages   _____
Dance   _____

9 Work with a partner. Compare and discuss your answers. Do you think a subject *should* be useful?

⦿ LANGUAGE DEVELOPMENT

UNLOCK ONLINE

EDUCATION NOUNS

1 Write the nouns from the box in the correct place in the table below. Use a dictionary to check the meaning of any new words.

> an office   a principal   a lecturer   a library   a teacher   a lab
> a college   a university   a class   a student   a graduate

places	people

PLURAL NOUNS

2 Some of the nouns below are singular (one thing) and some are plural (more than one thing). Write the words *singular* and *plural* in the gaps.

A _____   B _____

1 one school	→	some schools
2 one university	→	two universities
3 one business	→	many businesses
4 one person	→	twenty people

3 Match the words (1–4) in Exercise 2 to the rules (a–d) below.

a To make the plural form of a noun ending in *-s, -ch, -sh, -z* or *-x*, add *-es*.   _____

b Some plurals are irregular.   _____

c To make the plural form of a regular noun, add an *-s*.   _____

d To make the plural form of a noun ending in *consonant + -y*, delete the *-y* and add *-ies*.   _____

4 Write the plural forms of the nouns.

1 city ➔   _____
2 box ➔   _____
3 family ➔   _____
4 student ➔   _____
5 child ➔   _____
6 academy ➔   _____
7 teacher ➔   _____
8 man ➔   _____
9 coach ➔   _____
10 woman ➔   _____

CRITICAL THINKING

At the end of this unit, you will write a descriptive paragraph. Look at this unit's Writing task in the box below.

> Describe your education.

1 Look at the notes below about two of the students from Reading 2. Write the students' names at the top of the columns (A–B).

Name	A _____
(1) _____ What? _____	Art History
(2) _____	Princeford University
(3) _____	watch lectures online, download notes
(4) _____	talk to lecturers online, live near family and friends
(5) _____	whenever I want
(6) _____	because I enjoy it

B _____

Practical Business

Princeford University

lecture, library, work in an office

study with friends

Monday to Friday

because I want to have my own company in the future

2 Read the information in the notes above. Write the question words in the correct place. The first one has been done for you as an example.

> How?   When?   Why?   ~~What?~~   Who?   Where?

Using a *wh-* chart to generate ideas

When you are asked to describe something, it can be difficult to decide what to write. Using a *wh-* question planner can help. It breaks down the question into sections. This makes it easier to think of things to write about and helps you organize your thoughts.

3 Write information about your education in the *wh-* chart below.

What?	
Where?	
How?	
Who?	
When?	
Why?	

WRITING

GRAMMAR FOR WRITING

EXPLANATION

Subject pronouns

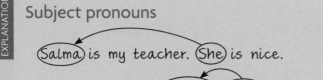

Salma is my teacher. She is nice.

I study with my friends. They are very clever.

Notice how we use *she* to replace *Salma* in the second sentence. When we replace a noun at the beginning of the sentence (a subject), we need to use a *subject pronoun*.

UNL⊘CK
ONLINE

1 Write the subject pronouns from the box in the correct place in the table below.

> I   he   you   it   they   she   you   we

singular subject pronouns	plural subject pronouns

2 Write a subject pronoun in each gap to complete the sentences. Use a capital letter at the start of a new sentence.

1 My sister is a doctor. _____ studies medicine.
2 All the medical students study hard. _____ want to pass the exams.
3 My college has over 12,000 students. _____ is quite big.
4 Maths and Engineering are practical subjects. _____ are very useful.
5 Oleg and I are studying the same course. _____ like the same subjects.
6 My brother goes to university. _____ studies English.

UNL⊘CK READING AND WRITING SKILLS 2

3 Read the paragraph below.

  1 Write subject pronouns in the gaps to complete the paragraph below. The first one has been done for you as an example.

  2 Circle the subject pronouns and the nouns that they refer to. Draw an arrow between each noun and its subject pronoun. The first one has been done for you as an example.

> I study (Physics) ¹_____(It)_____ is an interesting subject. My lecturer is called Amir. ²_____ is a very good teacher. There are thirty students on my course. Sometimes ³_____ all have a class together, but normally ⁴_____ work in small groups. I work with two other students: Lucy and Aleksander. ⁵_____ help me with my work. Lucy is very clever. ⁶_____ always gets good grades.

because and *so*

We use *because* and *so* to talk about reasons and results. We use *because* and *so* to join two sentences: a reason sentence and a result sentence.

reason: I want to work in different countries.

result: I'm studying English.

4 Look at the sentences below.

  1 Match the sentences in column A to the sentences in column B. The first one has been done for you as an example.

  2 Write *reason* and *result* in the gaps above the columns to show which sentences are the reason sentences and which are the result sentences.

A _____

  1 <u>I study Economics</u>.
  2 I study guitar.
  3 I study IT.
  4 I'm doing an apprenticeship in a restaurant.
  5 I'm going to university in Australia.

B _____

  a I want to design computer games.
  b I want to be a chef.
  c I want to learn English.
  d I love music.
  e <u>I want to work in a bank</u>.

5 Look at the sentences below with *because* and *so*. Underline the reason sentence and circle the result sentence.

  1 I'm studying English *because* I want to work in different countries.
  2 I want to work in different countries *so* I'm studying English.

6 What do you notice about the order of the sentences with *because* and *so*?

7 Join each pair of sentences in Exercise 4 to make one sentence with *because*. The first one has been done for you as an example.

1 I study Economics because I want to work in a bank.

2 _____

3 _____

4 _____

5 _____

8 Join each pair of sentences in Exercise 4 to make one sentence with *so*. The first one has been done for you as an example.

1 I want to work in a bank so I study Economics.

2 _____

3 _____

4 _____

5 _____

ACADEMIC WRITING SKILLS

EXPLANATION

Paragraph organization 2: topic, supporting and concluding sentences

A paragraph has a topic sentence, supporting sentences and a concluding sentence. We write a paragraph in this order:

1 The **topic sentence** describes what the paragraph is about. It is usually the first sentence in a paragraph.

2 The **supporting sentences** tell us more about the topic, and give details and examples. They are in the middle of the paragraph.

3 The **concluding sentence** ends the paragraph. It usually summarizes the main idea in the paragraph. Some short paragraphs do not have a concluding sentence.

1 Look at the paragraph below.

1 Underline the topic sentence and write *T* next to it.
2 Underline the supporting sentences and write *S* next to them.
3 Underline the concluding sentence and write *C* next to it.

> I went to the primary school opposite my home. It was a small school but very friendly. The teachers were very kind and all the students liked them. My father went to the school when he was young. I want to be a teacher because I enjoyed going to school.

2 Look at sentences (a–e) below.

1 Write *T* next to the topic sentence, *S* next to the supporting sentences and *C* next to the concluding sentence.

2 Put the sentences in order to make a paragraph. Number the topic sentence *1*, the supporting sentences *2* and the concluding sentence *3*.

   a I start classes at 9 am and finish at 3 pm. _____ _____

   b I study Physics at Adelaide University. _____ _____

   c I have classes and I study online. I also study in the library. _____ _____

   d I study Physics because the subject is interesting. _____ _____

   e There are 80 students on my course. We have some lectures together but normally we work in small groups. _____ _____

WRITING TASK

Describe your education.

1 Look at the sandwich paragraph planner below. A sandwich paragraph planner helps you organize the topic sentence, supporting sentences and concluding sentence of a paragraph.

PLAN

> TOPIC SENTENCE:

> SUPPORTING SENTENCE (1):

> SUPPORTING SENTENCE (2):

> SUPPORTING SENTENCE (3):

> CONCLUDING SENTENCE:

1 Write your topic sentence in the top section of the planner. Write about what you study and where you study.

2 Look at your notes from the Critical thinking section (page 62). Choose three important details about your education. Write three supporting sentences about these details in the middle sections of the planner.

3 Write your concluding sentence in the bottom section of the planner. Write about why you study your subject. Use *because* or *so* in your answer.

2 Use the sentences in the sandwich paragraph planner to write a paragraph.

3 Use the task checklist to review your paragraph for content and structure.

TASK CHECKLIST	✔
Have you written a paragraph about your education?	
Have you included information about what, where, how, who, when and why?	
Is there a topic sentence, supporting sentences and a concluding sentence in your paragraph?	
Have you used *because* or *so* to explain why you study your subject?	

4 Make any necessary changes to your paragraph.

5 Now use the language checklist to edit your paragraph for language errors which are common to A2 learners.

LANGUAGE CHECKLIST	✔
Have you used education nouns correctly?	
Have you used the correct form of plural nouns?	
Have you used the correct subject pronoun?	
Have you used *because* and *so* correctly?	

6 Make any necessary changes to your paragraph.

OBJECTIVES REVIEW

7 Check your objectives.

I can ...

watch and understand a video about education and learning.

very well — not very well

skim a text.

very well — not very well

write a paragraph with a topic sentence, supporting sentences and a concluding sentence.

very well — not very well

write a descriptive paragraph.

very well — not very well

WORDLIST

UNIT VOCABULARY		
class (n)	skill (n)	exchange (v)
college (n)	student (n)	join (v)
course (n)	subject (n)	look after (v)
degree (n)	support (n)	matter (v)
graduate (n)	teacher (n)	return (v)
lecture (n)	training (n)	train (v)
library (n)	university (n)	independent (adj)
notes (n)	apply (v)	local (adj)
office (n)	believe (v)	professional (adj)
project (n)	create (v)	similar (adj)

LEARNING OBJECTIVES

Watch and listen	Watch and understand a video about social media
Reading skills	Make inferences
Academic writing skills	Identify and write a topic sentence
Writing task	Write a one-sided opinion paragraph

THE INTERNET AND TECHNOLOGY

UNL⊘CK YOUR KNOWLEDGE

1 How much time do you spend on the internet every week?

2 What do you use the internet for? Complete the table below.

	never	sometimes	a lot
1 I look at photos.			
2 I listen to radio programmes.			
3 I search for information.			
4 I watch videos or TV.			
5 I check my bank account.			
6 I shop online.			
7 I play games.			
8 I chat to my friends.			

PREPARING TO WATCH

> **social media (n):** forms of media that allow people to communicate and share information using the internet

UNDERSTANDING KEY VOCABULARY

1 Read the dictionary definition of *social media* above. Circle the words in the box below that match the definition. Check the meaning of any new words in the glossary on page 195.

> blogs   magazines   social networking sites
> newspapers   TV   email

2 The video talks about four social media websites. Look at the company logos below. Which companies will the video talk about?

3 ▶ Watch the video and check your answers.

WHILE WATCHING

4 ▶ Watch again. Circle the best description of the topic of the video.

UNDERSTANDING MAIN IDEAS

   a How will social media change our lives in the future?

   b How has social media changed our lives?

5 ▶ Watch again. And number the descriptions (a–d) in the order that you hear them.

    a We can read blogs from all over the world.   _____

    b Social media means we can choose what we read and watch.   _____

    c Social media makes it easier to talk to our friends.   _____

    d Social media is very different from traditional media.   _____

6 Write words or numbers in the gaps to complete the summary below.

UNDERSTANDING DETAIL

> The Facebook story
>
> Mark Zuckerberg started Facebook in (1)_____ .
> (2)_____ million people use the website every day.
> He made the first version in a week and a (3)_____ .
> Soon, (4)_____ –thirds of Harvard students used it.
> Today, the number of users doubles every (5)_____
> months.

7 Look at the extract from the video script below and answer the questions.

MAKING INFERENCES

> With social media, we can share the videos, websites and music we like online. This means that we now have more control over what we watch, read and listen to.

    1 In what ways do social media give us more control over what we watch, read and listen?

    2 How is this different from traditional types of media, like TV or newspapers?

DISCUSSION

8 Work with a partner. Discuss the questions below.

    1 What types of social media do you use?

    2 What do you use social media for?

    3 Ten years from now, do you think Facebook will still be the number one social media website? Why / Why not?

READING 1

PREPARING TO READ

SCANNING TO
PREDICT CONTENT

1 Before you read, circle the title and subtitle in the web page opposite.

2 Circle the best description (a–c) of the topic of the web page.

   a the benefits (+) of the internet
   b the dangers (–) of the internet
   c why teenagers use the internet

3 Read the web page and check your answers.

WHILE READING

READING FOR
MAIN IDEAS

4 Read the text again. Underline the correct ending for each sentence.

   1 internet companies *ask you for information / take information without asking you.*
   2 internet companies show *different advertisements to different people / the same advertisements to everyone.*

READING FOR
DETAIL

UNL◌CK
ONLINE

5 Write the words from the box in the correct place in the table.

> your address   your interests   other websites you might like
> your gender (man/woman)   the way you use the internet
> your age   the websites you visit

A What do internet companies find out about you?	**B** What do internet companies guess about you?	**C** What do internet companies decide?

READING BETWEEN THE LINES

MAKING
INFERENCES

6 Look at the advertisements on the web page. What can you guess about the person using the website?

   1 Is it a man or a woman? _____
   2 How old is he/she? _____

7 Work with a partner. Compare and discuss your answers.

TEEN ZINE

HOME　BLOG　FILMS　MUSIC

Someone's always watching you online …

Did you know that when you surf the web, many websites put secret software on your computer? The software collects a large amount of information about you and sends it to internet companies. The companies find out where you live, what websites you visit and what you do online. With this information, they can guess other things about you. For example, they can guess if you are male or female*, how old you are and what kind of things you like. The companies use this information to decide which advertisements are best for you. Two people can go to the same website, but they will see different advertisements. For example, someone who likes sports could see an advertisement for trainers, and someone who likes films might see an advertisement for a cinema.

*male = a man, female = a woman

find out more

> **Making inferences**
>
> When we read, we often make inferences about a text. To make an inference, we think about what the author writes, the way they write it, and what you already know about the subject to make a guess about information that isn't in the text.

DISCUSSION

8 Read the three opinions about the topic of the web page (a–c). Circle the opinion you agree with most.

a I don't think companies should take any of this information from you – it's really bad.

b I don't see the problem. Companies need to make money some way – we get a lot of free things on the internet, and this is a good way to pay for them.

c I think it's great. If companies can show you advertisements for things you like, you can find out about new things.

9 Work with a partner. Compare and discuss your answers.

READING 2

PREPARING TO READ

UNDERSTANDING
KEY VOCABULARY

1 Match the words (1–8) to their definitions (a–h).

1 a grade	**a** a more polite way to say *fat*
2 download	**b** good at thinking of new ideas and making interesting things
3 educational	**c** copy computer programs, music, or information electronically
4 overweight	
5 improve	**d** a number or letter that shows how good your work is
6 imagination	
7 creative	**e** cause a change in someone or something
8 affect	**f** the ability to have ideas or pictures in your mind
	g get better or to make something better
	h related to education

UNLOCK READING AND WRITING SKILLS 2

2 Write the words from the box in the correct place in the table below.

advantage   disadvantage   benefit   negative   positive

+	–

WHILE READING

3 Read the text on page 76. Match the main ideas (1–4) to the paragraphs (A–D).

1 Are video games bad for our children? _____
2 Video games have positives and negatives. _____
3 Video games have some disadvantages. _____
4 Video games have some advantages. _____

READING FOR MAIN IDEAS

UNL⊘CK ONLINE

4 ~~Cross out~~ the advantages and disadvantages (1–8) that are not mentioned in the text.

READING FOR DETAIL

+	–
Video games ... 1 are creative. 2 improve the way children think. 3 teach children about money. 4 are fun.	Video games ... 5 can cause health problems. 6 are boring. 7 can make it difficult for children to learn to talk to people. 8 can be unsuitable for children.

READING BETWEEN THE LINES

5 What type of text is this?

a an essay   b a newspaper article   c a website

6 Who do you think is the author?

a a parent   b a journalist   c a student

IDENTIFYING TYPE

7 Work with a partner. Compare and discuss your answers.

A Do video games have a negative effect on our children? Today, our children spend more and more time online. Many children spend a lot of their free time playing online games on the internet. In the USA, 97% of teenagers play video games every week and children as young as five play video games regularly.

B For many people, video games are fun and educational. They have bright lights, funny cartoons and exciting stories. Everywhere you look, you can see children playing these games. They play on buses and trains, in restaurants and even at school. Video games also make you think in a creative way, and you have to move your hands and eyes quickly. This can improve the way that a child's brain works. Video games also make children use their imagination. The player has to do many creative things, like draw, tell stories and build things. Video games are also a good way to teach children about technology. They can learn about computers and how they work.

C However, a recent study suggests that video games can be bad for children. Firstly, children can download many online games for free. They don't need money, so they don't need to ask their parents. This means that their parents often don't know what they are playing. Children could play games that are violent or scary. Furthermore, many children spend too much time playing games on the computer. This can lead to health problems – children who spend too much time on the computer can become overweight. Also, if children spend too long on the computer instead of doing their homework, they can have problems at school and they can get bad grades. Video games can also affect children's social skills. Playing and working with friends is very important for children. It teaches them how to talk to other people. If children spend too much time playing by themselves online, they don't learn how to play with their friends.

D In conclusion, it seems clear that video games have some advantages and some disadvantages. On one hand, they are fun and have many educational benefits for children. On the other hand, they can cause problems with children's health and social skills.

DISCUSSION

8 Work with a partner. Answer the questions below.

1 Do you play video games? Why? / Why not?
2 Do you think that video games are bad for children? Why? / Why not?
3 Do you think spending a lot of time on the internet is good or bad for you?

⊙ LANGUAGE DEVELOPMENT

EXPLANATION

Compound nouns

In English, we often use certain words or groups of words together. When you learn new words, it is useful to learn the words that are used together.

A *compound noun* is a noun that is made of a group of two or three different words. Compound nouns are very common in English.

A *newspaper* is made of pieces of paper with the news printed on them.

A *bus stop* is the place where the bus stops for people to get on or off.

A *mother-in-law* is the mother of someone's husband or wife.

 UNLOCK ONLINE

1 Look at the examples in the box above and the statements (1–4) about compound nouns below. Cross out the incorrect statement.

   1 We write some compound nouns as two or three separate words.
   2 We always write compound nouns with a capital letter.
   3 We write some compound nouns with a hyphen.
   4 We write some compound nouns as one word.

2 Match the compound nouns (1–8) to their definitions (a–h).

   1 an online game
   2 a computer program
   3 a chat room
   4 a keyboard
   5 internet banking
   6 an email address
   7 a mobile phone
   8 a smartphone

   a a phone that you can take anywhere
   b a set of keys that you use to type
   c a mobile phone that can be used as a computer
   d the system that lets you use your bank account on the internet
   e a type of website that people use to talk to each other
   f a game on the internet
   g instructions that make a computer do something
   h an address for an email inbox

3 Use the compound nouns from Exercise 2 to complete the sentences.

   1 The _____ on my computer is broken. I can only type in capital letters.
   2 I've just bought a new _____ . I can use the internet anywhere now.
   3 What's your _____ ? I'll write to you next week.
   4 Give me your _____ number. I'll ring you soon.
   5 I love playing this _____ on my smartphone.
   6 Some people think that using _____ is dangerous for children.
   7 I've downloaded _____ to check my computer for viruses.
   8 I never visit the bank anymore. I always use _____ .

Giving opinions

In academic writing, we use the phrases *I think that*, *I believe that*, *It seems to me that* and *In my opinion* to talk about our opinions.

opinion: Video games are bad for children.

I think that video games are bad for children.
I believe that video games are bad for children.
It seems to me that video games are bad for children.
In my opinion, video games are bad for children.

4 Look at the phrases for giving opinions (a–d). Which phrase needs a comma at the end of it?

    a I think that
    b I believe that
    c It seems to me that
    d In my opinion

5 Write an adjective in each gap to make sentences that are true for you.

    1 Video games are _____ .
    2 Chat rooms are _____ .
    3 Social networking sites are _____ .
    4 internet banking is _____ .
    5 Smartphones are _____ .
    6 Watching videos online is _____ .

6 Rewrite the sentences in Exercise 5 to show that they are your opinion. Use the phrases in the box above.

1 _____

2 _____

3 _____

4 _____

5 _____

6 _____

CRITICAL THINKING

At the end of this unit, you will write a one-sided opinion paragraph. Look at this unit's Writing task in the box below.

> The internet has made our lives better. Do you agree or disagree?

Analyzing a question

Before you answer a question, it is important to analyze exactly what the question asks you to do. You can then decide what to write in order to answer the question correctly.

1 Match each essay question (1 or 2) to the correct way to answer it (a or b).

ANALYZE

  1 How has the internet made our lives better?
  2 The internet has made our lives better. Do you agree or disagree?
  a Give your opinion about whether the internet has made our lives better or worse and give examples to support your argument.
  b Describe the ways that the internet has made our lives better.

2 Look at the advantages and disadvantages of the internet (1–10). Write them in the correct place in the table on page 80.

EVALUATE

  1 The computer could get a virus.
  2 You can chat to your friends and see their photos.
  3 You can find all different kinds of information.
  4 You can waste a lot of time.
  5 Some people can experience online bullying.
  6 You can go shopping or check your bank accounts from home.
  7 A lot of information online is not reliable.
  8 You can read news and stories from all around the world.
  9 Young children could read or see unsuitable information.
  10 People can get addicted.

advantages	disadvantages

3 Work with a partner. Add two more points to each column.

WRITING

GRAMMAR FOR WRITING

and, also and *too*

We use the linkers *and, also* and *too* to add information. Using linkers makes our writing better and easier to understand.

We use *and* to join two sentences together.

> My sister uses her computer a lot. She has a smartphone.
> My sister uses her computer a lot **and** she has a smartphone.

We use *also* and *too* to connect the ideas in two separate sentences.

> My sister uses her computer a lot. She **also** has a smartphone.
> My sister uses her computer a lot. She has a smartphone, **too**.

Notice how we put *also* before the main verb. We put *too* at the end of the sentence, and we put a comma before it.

1 Join each pair of sentences to make one sentence with *and*. The first one has been done for you as an example.

1 Video games are boring. They can make you overweight.
<u>Video games are boring and they can make you overweight.</u>

2 You can share photos. You can talk to your friends.
_____

3 I use internet banking. I check my emails.
_____

4 My friends send me videos. I watch them on my phone.
_____

5 I often go shopping on the internet. I pay with my credit card.
_____

2 Rewrite the sentences below. Put the words in brackets in the correct place.

1 Many people download music. (also)
_____

2 I write a blog about travelling. (too)
_____

3 I read the newspapers online. (also)
_____

4 Children can get bullied online. (too)
_____

5 I look at maps on my smartphone. (also)
_____

EXPLANATION

but and *however*

We use the linkers *but* and *however* to talk about opposite or different information or ideas.

> My children play video games. They do their homework and do sports.
> My children play video games **but** they do their homework and do sports.
> My children play video games. **However,** they do their homework and do sports.

Notice how we use *but* to join two sentences into one sentence. We use *however* at the start of a new sentence, followed by a comma.

---

3 Join each pair of sentences to make one sentence with *but*. Then rewrite each pair of sentences using *however*. The first one has been done for you as an example.

1 The internet is very useful. It can be dangerous.
a <u>The internet is very useful but it can be dangerous.</u>
b <u>The internet is very useful. However, it can be dangerous.</u>

2 Many computer games are fun. Some online games are a waste of time.

a _____

b _____

3 I use internet banking. I sometimes forget my password.

a _____

b _____

4 I use the internet on my smartphone. Sometimes it is very slow.

a _____

b _____

ACADEMIC WRITING SKILLS

Topic sentences

In a paragraph, the topic sentence tells you the main idea of the paragraph. The topic sentence is usually the first sentence in a paragraph.

Look at the example below.

topic sentence

<u>There are many advantages and disadvantages to the internet.</u> On one hand, you can find information quickly and keep in touch with your friends. On the other hand, companies can use your private details and it can be dangerous for children.

1 Look at Reading 2 (page 76) and underline the topic sentences in paragraphs A, B, C and D.

2 In each paragraph (a–d) below, the topic sentence is missing. Match the topic sentences (1–4) to the correct paragraph.

1 Social networking sites make it easy to keep in touch with your friends.
2 Smartphones can be expensive.
3 Information on the internet is not reliable.
4 You can access information from all over the world.

a It is easy to spend a lot of money. Contracts for the phones can also cost a lot of money. It is important to be careful and pay attention to what you spend.

b You can read newspapers, magazines and blogs from many different countries. You can even translate information from other languages using a translation website. It is easy to find out what is happening anywhere you want.

c You can look at your friends' photos and see what they are doing. Your friends can send you messages and links. You can also share interesting articles and videos.

d Anyone can publish articles and information online. Websites often do not say who has written an article or where they got their facts. People can write things that are not true.

WRITING TASK

> The internet has made our lives better. Do you agree or disagree?

1 Look at the question above. Do you agree or disagree?

2 Circle the topic sentence that is best to describe your opinion.

   1 The internet has made our lives better.
   2 The internet has made our lives worse.

3 Look at the table in the Critical thinking section (page 80). Circle the three ideas that are best to support your argument.

4 Look at the paragraph planner below.

   1 Write your topic sentence in the correct place in the planner.
   2 Write your three supporting ideas in the correct place in the planner.

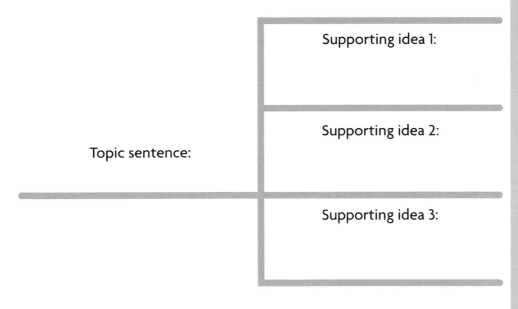

Topic sentence:

Supporting idea 1:

Supporting idea 2:

Supporting idea 3:

5 Write a concluding sentence.

_____

6 Write the first draft of your paragraph. Use linkers to connect your ideas.

7 Use the task checklist to review your paragraph for content and structure.

TASK CHECKLIST	✔
Have you answered the question correctly?	
Have you included a topic sentence?	
Have you included three supporting ideas?	
Have you included a concluding sentence?	
Have you used linkers to connect your ideas?	

8 Make any necessary changes to your paragraph.

9 Now use the language checklist to edit your paragraph for language errors which are common to A2 learners.

LANGUAGE CHECKLIST	✔
Have you used compound nouns correctly?	
Have you used the correct sentence order with the phrases *I think that, I believe that, it seems to me that* and *in my opinion*?	
Have you used *and, also* and *too* correctly?	
Have you used *but* and *however* correctly?	

10 Make any necessary changes to your paragraph.

OBJECTIVES REVIEW

11   Check your objectives.

I can ...

watch and understand a
video about social media.   very   not very
                      well   well

make inferences.

                     very   not very
                     well   well

identify and write a topic
sentence.   very   not very
                     well   well

write a one-sided opinion
paragraph.   very   not very
                     well   well

WORDLIST

UNIT VOCABULARY		
blog (n)	internet banking (n)	improve (v)
chat room (n)	keyboard (n)	creative (adj)
computer program (n)	magazine (n)	educational (adj)
disadvantage (n)	mobile phone (n)	overweight (adj)
email (n)	online game (n)	
email address (n)	social networking	
grade (n)	site (n)	
imagination (n)	download (v)	

LEARNING OBJECTIVES

Watch and listen	Watch and understand a video about codes
Reading skills	Read for main ideas
Academic writing skills	Identify and write supporting sentences
Writing task	Write a descriptive paragraph

LANGUAGE AND COMMUNICATION

UNIT 5

UNLOCK YOUR KNOWLEDGE

1 Match the symbols (1–6) to their meanings (a–f).

a parking   b restaurant   c lift   d stop   e hotel   f no smoking

WATCH AND LISTEN

PREPARING TO WATCH

UNDERSTANDING KEY VOCABULARY

1 Before you watch, match the words (1–8) to their definitions (a–h).

1 simple
2 protect
3 complicated
4 develop
5 message
6 type
7 invent
8 original

a the earliest or first form of something
b design or make something new
c not difficult to do or understand
d write something using a keyboard
e with many different parts and difficult to understand
f keep someone or something safe
g work on something to make it better
h a piece of written or spoken information that one person gives to another

PREVIEWING

2 Look at the dictionary entry for the word *code* and the photographs from the video. What do you think the video will be about?

> **code (n):** a set of letters, numbers or signs used to share secret information between certain people and make sure that other people can't understand it

a the history of codes
b how to write code for computers
c how to learn a language

3 ▶ Watch the video and check your answers.

WHILE WATCHING

UNDERSTANDING MAIN IDEAS

4 ▶ Watch again. Number the ideas (a–c) in the order that you hear them.

a computer codes _____
b a Roman alphabet code _____
c the Enigma code machine _____

5 Circle the correct words to complete the sentences.

1 The Ancient Romans used *the alphabet / number codes* to send messages.
2 The Ancient Romans used pots of water and *lights / sounds* to communicate.
3 *In the 1900s, / In 1919,* codes became more complicated.
4 The Enigma machine looked like a *computer / typewriter*.
5 The Enigma machine had *thousands / billions* of possible codes.
6 The people who worked with the Enigma machine helped make the first *computer passwords / computers*.
7 Today, we use codes for computers, mobile phones and the *alphabet / internet*.
8 *Codes / Emails* keep our private information safe online.

6 ▶ Watch again. Put the sentences (a–f) in order to explain how Romans used water for codes.

a The soldiers see the second light.   _____
b All soldiers read the same message at the same time.   _____
c The soldiers start to pour water out of the pot.   _____
d The soldiers stop pouring water.   _____
e The soldiers see the first light.   _____
f Every pot of water has the same list of messages in it.   _____

7 Circle the correct definition of the word *break*.

a to stop working or to make something stop working
b to make a sudden, short noise

8 What do you think the phrase *break a code* means? Circle the correct definition.

a to write a code that nobody understands
b to work out and understand what a code means

DISCUSSION

9 Work with a partner. Discuss the questions below.

1 How is learning a language like learning a code?
2 Do you enjoy learning new languages? Why / Why not?
3 What are the secrets of being a good language learner?

PREPARING TO READ

1 Circle the correct definition for each word.

1 a letter
   a a type of language
   b one of the symbols (for example *a, j, p*) that we use to write words

2 an alphabet
   a a set of letters used for writing a language
   b a set of numbers used by a bank

3 a symbol
   a a sign or object that is used to mean something
   b a large object that is used to move something

4 main
   a least important or smallest
   b most important or largest

5 extra
   a more or more than usual
   b less or less than usual

6 explain
   a make something difficult to understand
   b make something easy to understand by telling someone about it

7 a text message
   a a message in writing sent by post
   b a message in writing sent on a mobile phone to another

2 Match the symbols and letters (1–6) to the languages (a–f).

1 안녕하세요   **a** Arabic _____

2 你好   **b** English _____

3 العربية   **c** Turkish _____

4 𝓜erhaba   **d** Chinese _____

5 こんにちは   **e** Korean _____

6 **hello**   **f** Japanese _____

3 Which of the languages (a–f) in Exercise 2 use alphabets, and which languages use pictures? Write the languages in the correct place in the table below.

alphabet	pictures

4 Read the text on page 92 and check your answers.

WHILE READING

5 Read the text again. Write the words from the box in the gaps to complete the summary below.

READING FOR
MAIN IDEAS

UNLOCK
ONLINE

> Turkish   change   letters   learn   emoticons
> two   languages   symbols

There are (1)_____ types of writing systems. Picture systems use (2)_____ to show meaning. They have lots of pictures that you have to (3)_____ . Alphabet systems use (4)_____ . Languages sometimes (5)_____ their writing systems. Korean and (6)_____ have both changed their writing systems. People use symbols in many (7)_____ . Many people use (8)_____ to show how they feel.

WRITING SYSTEMS

Topic overview

There are two main kinds of writing systems*.
- alphabets
- pictures

Key facts

- First writing system: 3,000 BCE (Before Common Era)
- Egyptian writing system: 2,500 BCE
- First alphabet system: 2,000–1,000 BCE
- Persian writing system: 1,500 BCE
- Chinese writing system: from 1,000 BCE
- Arabic alphabet system: from about 400 CE

Alphabet writing systems

Some writing systems use alphabets. Alphabet writing systems use letters to tell you what sounds to make. Arabic and English both use an alphabet. There are 26 letters in the English alphabet and 28 letters in the Arabic alphabet. The first alphabet started in the Middle East 3,000 years ago. The English and Arabic alphabets both come from this alphabet.

Picture or symbol writing systems

Some writing systems use pictures or symbols to show the meaning of words. Picture writing started 5,000 years ago in the Middle East. Modern Chinese uses a similar system today. Japanese also uses some of the symbols from the Chinese picture system. For example, the Chinese word for fish is 'yu' and the Japanese word is 'sakana', but both languages write it the same way. There are thousands of symbols in picture writing systems – you have to learn 4,000 symbols to read Chinese.

Writing systems and change

Languages sometimes change their writing systems. Before 1423, the Korean language used the Chinese picture system. In 1423, the Koreans invented their own alphabet system. Now Korean uses an alphabet system. Turkey also changed its writing system. Before 1928, Turkish used the Arabic alphabet. Today it uses an alphabet like English, but with some extra symbols, like 'ş' and 'ç'.

Do you use symbols?

Today, in many languages, we use symbols to explain what we mean. For example, many people use symbols like ☺ and ☹ when they write text messages or emails. These symbols show how we feel. They are called emoticons because they tell people about our emotions.

See also:
Ancient civilisations: Middle East, China
Languages: Arabic, Chinese, English, Japanese, Korean, Turkish

* writing system: the way of writing a language

Fish / Fish / Fish

6 Read the text again and answer the questions below.

1 When was the first writing system invented? _____
2 Where was the first picture writing system? _____
3 How many symbols do you need to learn to read Chinese? _____
4 How many years old is the oldest alphabet? _____
5 When did Korea change its writing system? _____
6 When did Turkey change its writing system? _____

UNLOCK READING AND WRITING SKILLS 2

READING BETWEEN THE LINES

7 Where would you find this text?

    a in a novel   **b** in a newspaper   **c** in an online encyclopaedia

8 Does the text contain facts or opinions? _____

RECOGNIZING TEXT TYPE

DISCUSSION

9 Work with a partner. Discuss the questions below.

    1 Which writing system does your language use?
    2 How many symbols or letters are there in your language?
    3 Is it easier to learn a second language with the same writing system as your first language?
    4 Do you ever use emoticons? Why / Why not?

READING 2

PREPARING TO READ

1 Match the words (1–5) to their definitions (a–e).

UNDERSTANDING KEY VOCABULARY

    1 a reason   **a** start to be something
    2 describe   **b** the fact that explains why something happens
    3 become   **c** use an object, like a switch, to operate a machine
    4 natural   **d** say or write what someone or something is like
    5 control   **e** normal or expected

2 Read the title of the article on page 95. Why would someone read this article?

SCANNING TO PREDICT CONTENT

    a to find instructions about how to do something
    b to find information for an essay or exam

3 What do you think the article will be about?

    a the way that languages change
    b the different types of languages

4 Read the article and check your answers.

WHILE READING

5 Find and underline the topic sentence of each paragraph. Which paragraph (A–C) contains the information (1–3) below? Circle the answers.

READING FOR MAIN IDEAS

    1 the arguments for and against language change   A   B   C
    2 how English is changing   A   B   C
    3 reasons for language change   A   B   C

Reading for main ideas

When we read, it is important to understand the main ideas in the text. In a text, each paragraph usually has one main idea. We can find the main ideas of each paragraph by reading the topic sentences. The topic sentence tells us the main idea of the paragraph. It is usually the first sentence in the paragraph.

READING
FOR DETAIL

UNL⊙CK
ONLINE

6 Read the article again and check your answers.

7 Read the article again and write true (T) or false (F) next to the statements below.

1 The English language has not changed in the last 500 years. _____

2 The word *website* is older than the word *internet*. _____

3 L'Académie Française decides what is correct and incorrect in French. _____

4 There are organizations in France, Indonesia and Spain that want to protect their languages. _____

8 Look at the words in italics in the text. Write them in the correct place in the table below.

words to talk about new types of technology	words from other languages	words that started as slang

READING BETWEEN THE LINES

MAKING
INFERENCES

9 Work with a partner. Look at paragraph C.

1 Underline the sentences that say language change is a positive thing. Write *P* above the sentences.

2 Underline the sentences that say language change is a negative thing. Write *N* above the sentences.

10 Which argument do you agree with? Explain your answers.

♠ home

Language change: a study guide

A   English is always changing. The English that people used 500 years ago is very different to the English we use now. Even in the last fifty years, English has changed. New words are entering our language all the time. The words *internet, email* and *mobile phone* are only twenty years old. The word *website* is even younger. We only started using it fifteen years ago. But what causes languages to change? And is language change a positive or a negative thing?

B   There are many reasons that languages change. One reason is that technology changes. We use new words for new types of technology. Thirty years ago, we only used the word *mouse* in English to describe an animal. Today, the word *mouse* also means the object you use to control a computer. Another important reason for language change is communication between different countries and cultures. For instance, English uses words like *sugar* from Arabic, *shampoo* from Hindi and *yoghurt* from Turkish. Languages also change because young people create their own way of talking that is different from their parents. Teenagers often use new slang – informal words and phrases – to talk to their friends. Some slang gets forgotten, but other slang words become part of normal, everyday language. Words like *bus* and *rock music* started as slang, but now they are in the dictionary and everyone uses them.

C   But is language change a good thing or a bad thing? Some people think that we should stop languages from changing. They think that they need to protect their language or it will die or become worse. In France, there is an organization called L'Académie Française that decides what is correct and what is incorrect in French. They look at the new words that people are using and decide whether they are good French or not. There are also organizations like this in other countries, such as Indonesia and Spain. However, other people believe that language change is a natural thing and shouldn't be stopped. They think that it is normal that languages change over time. They think that languages need to change to stay modern and interesting.

DISCUSSION

11   Work with a partner. Discuss the questions below.

1   Do you know any words in your language that young people use more than the older generation?

2   Is technology changing the way people speak or write in your country?

3   Do you know any words in your language that come from English or another language?

4   Do you know any words in English which come from your language?

EXPLANATION

Countable and uncountable nouns

Countable nouns are nouns that we can count.

one word → two words

Uncountable nouns are nouns that we cannot count. Uncountable nouns often refer to food, liquids and ideas.

~~informations~~ → information

UNLOCK ONLINE

1   Look at the words in the box. Are they countable or uncountable nouns? Write them in the correct place in the table below. The first one in each column has been done for you as an example.

> ~~word~~   ~~information~~   job   work   food   health   sign   transport   technology   computer   symbol   water   money   system

countable nouns	uncountable nouns
word	information

EXPLANATION

Articles: *a*, *an* or no article

We use *a* or *an* before:
– a singular countable noun

   a word

We use *a* before:
– a noun that starts with a consonant

   a sentence

We use *an* before:
– a noun that starts with a vowel (*a, e, i, o, u*)

   an example

We do not use *a* or *an* before:
– a plural countable noun

   words

– an uncountable noun

   information

2 Write *a*, *an* or *X* (no article) in the gaps to complete the sentences below.

1 I often use slang words for _____ money.
2 In a cinema, there is usually _____ sign for the exit.
3 There are many foreign words in English to describe _____ food.
4 People use _____ codes to write computer programs.
5 I check my email in _____ internet café.
6 We often use _____ symbol to say *No Smoking*.
7 We often use new words to describe _____ technology.

CRITICAL THINKING

At the end of this unit, you will write a descriptive paragraph. Look at this unit's Writing task in the box below.

How is your language different from 50 years ago? Describe how people speak and write your language has changed.

Using an ideas map to plan supporting ideas and examples

When we answer a question, we need to think of examples or give evidence. An ideas map helps us see how main ideas, supporting ideas and examples or evidence fit together.

1 Look at the ideas map about English below. Write the words from the box in the gaps (1–5) to complete the ideas map.

smartphone   hip-hop   R&B   internet   food

A _____   B _____   C _____

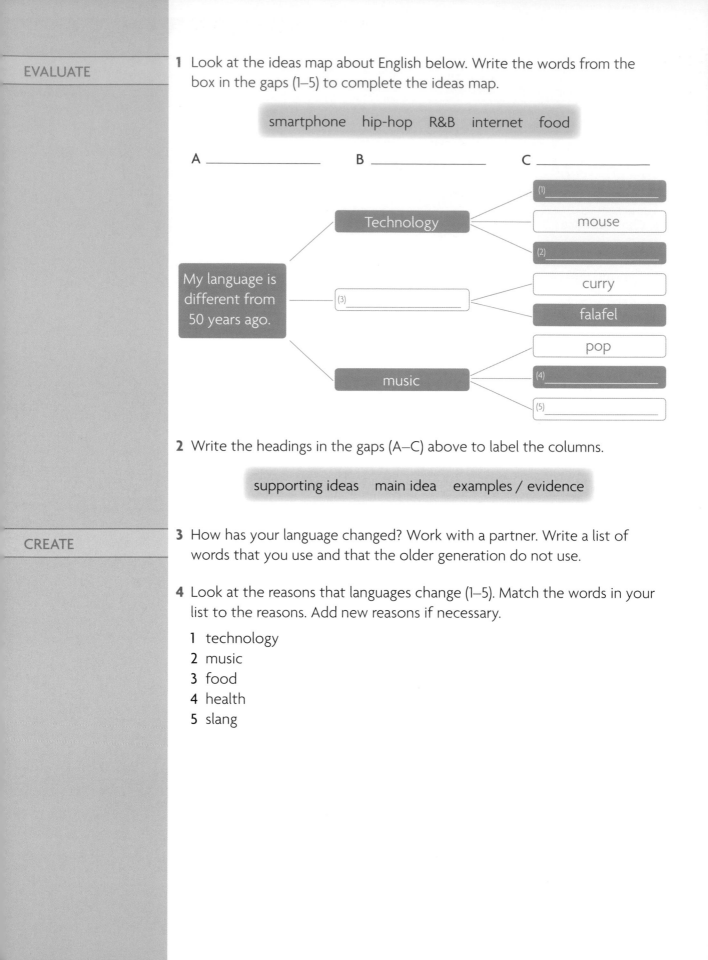

2 Write the headings in the gaps (A–C) above to label the columns.

supporting ideas   main idea   examples / evidence

3 How has your language changed? Work with a partner. Write a list of words that you use and that the older generation do not use.

4 Look at the reasons that languages change (1–5). Match the words in your list to the reasons. Add new reasons if necessary.

1 technology
2 music
3 food
4 health
5 slang

WRITING

GRAMMAR FOR WRITING

EXPLANATION

Quantifiers: *some, many, a lot of, a few, a little*

We use *quantifiers* before a noun to say *how many* or *how much* there is of something.

Some languages use alphabets.

We use different quantifiers with countable and uncountable nouns.

quantifiers with countable nouns	quantifiers with uncountable nouns
a lot of many some a few	*a lot of some a little*

UNLOCK ONLINE

1 Write the quantifiers from the table above in the gaps below to show when we use them. More than one option is possible.

   a to talk about a large amount, we use _____

   b to talk about a small amount, we use _____

2 Circle the correct words to complete the sentences (1–5). Think about the meaning of the quantifiers and the grammar.

   1 There are *a lot of / a few* symbols in the Chinese alphabet.
   2 *A few / A little* languages use picture writing systems.
   3 *A little / A lot of* people learn a foreign language at school.
   4 *Many / A few* languages use alphabets. There are hundreds of them.
   5 *A few / Some* technology causes languages to change.

3 Use phrases from columns A and B with *some, many, a lot, a few* and *a little* to write sentences that are true for you.

A	B
My school has	interesting people.
I can read	English words.
I know	French words.
I can spell	good technology.
My language uses	picture symbols.

1 _____

2 _____

3 _____

4 _____

5 _____

ACADEMIC WRITING SKILLS

Supporting sentences

The *topic sentence* explains the main idea of a paragraph. The *supporting sentences* in a paragraph give us more information about the topic sentence. They explain or give more information about the main idea.

Topic sentence

People have used codes throughout history.

Supporting sentence

The Romans used alphabet codes.

1 Match the topic sentences (1–5) to the supporting sentences (a–e).

  1 Children often talk differently at school.
  2 People from different regions in England have different accents.
  3 Deaf people, or people who can't hear well, use sign language.
  4 Some people think that language change is bad.
  5 Translation can be quite difficult.

  a They think that we should have grammar and language academies to protect languages.
  b Many languages use set phrases and idioms that you can't translate.
  c People from the north-east often have a strong accent.
  d They use different words with their friends than with their family.
  e They use their hands to make signs that explain different words and ideas.

Giving examples: *like, such as* and *for example*

In a supporting sentence, we often give examples to support the main idea. We use *like, such as* and *for example* to give an example, or a list of examples.

Turkish uses an English alphabet but it also uses extra symbols, like 'ş' and 'ç'.

Turkish uses an English alphabet but it also uses extra symbols, such as 'ş' and 'ç'.

Turkish uses an English alphabet but it also uses extra symbols – for example, 'ş' and 'ç'.

Notice how we use a comma before *like* and *such as*. We use a comma after *for example*.

2 Rewrite the sentences below. Put the words in brackets in the correct place and use *like*, *such as* or *for example* with the correct punctuation.

1   There are many new words for technology in English. (iPhone, laptop)
<u>There are many new words for technology in English,</u>
<u>like iPhone and laptop.</u>

2   There are a few Japanese words in English. (karaoke, sushi)

_____

3   There are a lot of words for kinds of music in English. (hip-hop, reggae)

_____

4   There are some words for new sports in English. (jogging)

_____

WRITING TASK

> How is your language different from 50 years ago? Describe how people speak and write your language has changed.

1 Look at your notes in the Critical thinking section (page 98).

1   Choose three reasons for language change. (You can add to or change your reasons if necessary.) These will be your supporting sentences.
2   For each reason, choose two or three words from your list. These will be your examples.

2 Use your notes to complete the ideas map below.

PLAN

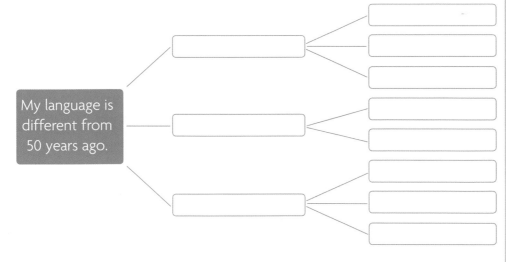

3 Look at the ideas map. Write your topic sentence.

_____

4 Look at the ideas map again. Write your supporting sentences. Add your examples using *like*, *such as* and *for example*.

_____

_____

_____

WRITE A
FIRST DRAFT

EDIT

5 Write the first draft of your paragraph.

6 Use the task checklist to review your paragraph for content and structure.

TASK CHECKLIST	✔
Have you written a topic sentence?	
Have you included three reasons for language change?	
Have you included examples for each reason?	
Have you used *like*, *such as* and *for example* to give examples?	

7 Make any necessary changes to your paragraph.

8 Now use the language checklist to edit your paragraph for language errors which are common to A2 learners.

LANGUAGE CHECKLIST	✔
Have you used countable and uncountable nouns correctly?	
Have you used articles *a*, *an* or *no article* correctly?	
Have you used quantifiers correctly?	

9 Make any necessary changes to your paragraph.

OBJECTIVES REVIEW

10 Check your objectives.

I can ...

watch and understand a
video about codes.

very
well

not very
well

read for main ideas.

very
well

not very
well

identify and write
supporting sentences.

very
well

not very
well

write a descriptive
paragraph.

very
well

not very
well

WORDLIST

UNIT VOCABULARY		
alphabet (n)	become (v)	type (v)
code (n)	control (v)	complicated (adj)
letter (n)	describe (v)	extra (adj)
message (n)	develop (v)	main (adj)
reason (n)	explain (v)	natural (adj)
symbol (n)	invent (v)	original (adj)
text message (n)	protect (v)	simple (adj)

LEARNING OBJECTIVES

Watch and listen	Watch and understand a video about people who follow storms
Reading skills	Use knowledge to predict content
Academic writing skills	Write a topic sentence to describe a graph and use data to support ideas
Writing task	Write sentences to describe a graph

WEATHER AND CLIMATE | UNIT 6

UNLOCK YOUR KNOWLEDGE

1 Match the types of weather to the photographs (1–4).

snow (n)   sun (n)   rain (n)   wind (n)

2 What is your favourite weather? Why?

3 What is your least favourite weather? Why?

WATCH AND LISTEN

PREPARING TO WATCH

UNDERSTANDING
KEY VOCABULARY

1 Match the words (1–5) to their meanings (a–e).

1 a season   **a** damage something so badly that it cannot be used
2 destroy   or does not exist
3 predict   **b** an extremely strong wind that moves in a circle
4 a tornado   **c** say what you think will happen in the future
5 dangerous   **d** a period of the year when a particular
                             thing happens
                 e describes something that could harm you

2 Read the dictionary definitions of the words below. What do you think
the word *stormchaser* means?

> **chase (v):** to run after something and try to catch it
> **storm (n):** very bad weather with a lot of rain, snow or wind

a someone who tells people a tornado is coming
b someone who follows tornadoes
c someone who paints storms

3 ▶ Watch the video and check your answers.

WHILE WATCHING

4 ▶ Watch again. Circle the correct words to complete the sentences.

1 Tornadoes *only / mostly* happen in the USA.
2 *Some / All* large tornadoes are dangerous.
3 Tornadoes *never / sometimes* kill people.
4 Stormchasers follow tornadoes for *different / the same* reasons.
5 Stormchasers' work *is / is not* important.
6 Stormchasers can help us to *get energy from tornadoes / save lives in the future*.

5 ▶ Watch again. Circle the reasons that stormchasers do their job.

a They want to study tornadoes, and get more information.
b They want to test their cars.
c They want to take pictures and videos.
d They think tornadoes aren't dangerous.

6 Are the statements below about Josh Wurman or Reed Timmer? Write J (Josh) or R (Reed) next to the statements.

1 He is a scientist. _____
2 He works with a large team of helpers. _____
3 He works with a few friends. _____
4 He uses advanced technology, like radar, to find tornadoes. _____
5 He uses the internet and an ordinary 4x4 car to follow tornadoes. _____
6 He has a special truck. _____
7 He makes videos and sells them to TV companies. _____

7 Do you think Reed Timmer enjoys his job?

8 How do you know?

DISCUSSION

9 Work with a partner. Discuss the questions.

1 Tornadoes are an example of dangerous weather. What other kinds of dangerous weather do you know?
2 Does your country have dangerous weather? What kind?

UNDERSTANDING
MAIN IDEAS

UNDERSTANDING
DETAIL

MAKING
INFERENCES

PREPARING TO READ

UNDERSTANDING
KEY VOCABULARY

1 Write the words from the box in the gaps to complete the definitions (1–5).

cover   damage   cause   huge   almost

1 _____ means to cause harm or injury.
2 When we _____ something , we put something over the top of it.
3 _____ means very large.
4 _____ means nearly.
5 _____ means make something happen.

2 Match the weather words (1–5) to the definitions (a–e).

1 natural disaster
2 a flood
3 lightning
4 thunder
5 temperature

a how hot or cold something is
b an event caused by extreme weather such as rain, storms or heat that damages the environment or causes loss of life
c the loud noise in the sky that you hear during a storm
d the sudden, bright light in the sky during a storm
e a large amount of water that covers an area that is usually dry

WHILE READING

READING FOR
MAIN IDEAS

UNLOCK
ONLINE

3 Read the text opposite. Circle the statement that gives the most important idea in each paragraph.

1 Paragraph A
   a Extreme weather is unusual and can cause natural disasters.
   b Extreme weather can take place over an hour.
2 Paragraph B
   a Hurricanes are sometimes called cyclones.
   b Hurricanes are huge, dangerous storms.
3 Paragraph C
   a In a heat wave, temperatures are hotter than normal.
   b Some people in the UK like heat waves.
4 Paragraph D
   a In 1999, there were floods in Nepal.
   b Floods happen when there is too much rain.
5 Paragraph E
   a A sandstorm is a storm with a lot of wind and dust.
   b It is difficult to drive a car in a sandstorm.

A Extreme weather

Extreme weather is when the weather is very different from normal. Extreme weather can take place over an hour, a day or a long period of time. It can be dangerous and, in some cases, it can cause natural disasters.

B Hurricane

A hurricane is a type of storm. These storms are also called cyclones or typhoons. In North and Central America they are called hurricanes, in the North Pacific they are called typhoons, and in the Indian Ocean and South Pacific they are called cyclones. These storms are huge: they can be over 500 kilometres wide. They start at sea and move towards land. When they come to land, they bring thunder, lightning, strong winds and very heavy rain. They can be very dangerous and destroy buildings and even kill people.

C Heat waves and droughts

A heat wave is when there are high temperatures and it is much hotter than normal. In many areas, heat waves are not a problem. In the UK, temperatures only reach around 30 °C in a heat wave, and many people enjoy the hot weather. However, in some places, heat waves can cause droughts. In a drought, there is not enough water for farmers to grow food. In some cases, people die because they don't have enough water to drink. Droughts are common in many countries in Africa, but in the last ten years, droughts also happened in Afghanistan, China and Iran.

D Rain storm

Too much rain can cause floods. Floods can destroy buildings and kill people. They can also destroy plants and food, which can mean that there is not enough food for people to eat. In 1999, there were very bad floods in India, Nepal, and other parts of Asia. In Bangladesh, almost half the country was covered in water. Thousands of homes were damaged and hundreds of people died.

E Sandstorm

A sandstorm is a large storm of dust and sand with strong winds. They can be very dangerous. It is difficult to travel by car because people can't see anything. Even walking can be difficult. Sandstorms are common in the Middle East and China. One of the worst sandstorms was in Iraq in 2011 when a storm lasted a whole week, causing many people to have breathing problems.

4 Choose the correct ending for each sentence (1–4).

1 Hurricanes move from
  a land to sea.
  b sea to land.

2 Heatwaves are
  a sometimes a problem.
  b always a problem.

3 Bangladesh had
  a a very big flood in 1999.
  b no floods in 1999.

4 The Middle East and China
  a are the only places with sandstorms.
  b have a lot of sandstorms.

READING BETWEEN THE LINES

5 What type of text is this?

  a an extract from a newspaper
  b an extract from a textbook
  c an extract from a novel

6 Who would be interested in reading this text?

  a a biology student
  b a history student
  c a geography student

7 What kind of information is included in the text?

  a facts
  b opinions

DISCUSSION

8 Work with a partner. Discuss the questions below.

  1 Do you prefer hot or cold weather?
  2 What is the worst weather you have experienced?
  3 Has the weather in your country changed in recent years?

READING 2

PREPARING TO READ

1 You are going to read about the Sahara desert. Before you read, try to answer the questions below.

1 Where is the Sahara desert?
  a South Africa
  b North Africa
  c Central Asia

2 What is the weather like there?
  a hot and dry
  b cold and wet
  c hot and wet

Using your knowledge to predict content

We understand something better if we can connect it with what we already know. Before you read something, think about what you know about the topic first. This gets you ready for reading and helps you understand.

2 Read the article on page 112 and check your answers.

3 Match the words in the box to the definitions (1–10).

UNDERSTANDING KEY VOCABULARY

> protect   a desert   rainfall   survive   an expert
> a shock   signal   last   decide   careful

1   someone who has a lot of skill in something or a lot of knowledge about something _____
2   when a person tries hard not to make a mistake _____
3   a large, often hot, dry area of land with very few plants _____
4   continue to live in a difficult or dangerous situation _____
5   a bad surprise _____
6   continue for a particular period of time _____
7   make a movement or sound to tell someone to do something

_____

8   the amount of rain that falls over a period of time _____
9   choose something after thinking about the possibilities _____
10   keep someone or something safe from danger _____

4 Write the nouns from the box in the correct place in the table. Use a dictionary to check the meaning of any new words.

> a tyre   a snake   a blanket   a jumper   trousers
> a scorpion   a mirror   a hole

things	animals

Surviving the Sea of Sand
How to stay alive in the Sahara Desert
Brad Rogers

A Can you imagine a sea of sand three times bigger than India? This is the Sahara desert, the largest desert in the world. It covers 11 countries in North Africa and is over 9 million km². That's more than 25% of Africa.

B In the Sahara, temperatures are very different during the day and at night. It is much hotter during the day than at night. It is very hot during the day – the hottest time is between 2 pm and 4 pm, when temperatures rise to 33 °C. But it is very cold at night – the coldest time is at 4 am, when temperatures fall to -1 °C. The Sahara is very dry. The average rainfall in a year is only 70 mm. That's just one cup of rain in a whole year.

C Because of the extreme temperatures in the desert, it is a very difficult place to survive. Brad Johnson, our survival expert, has some tips:

D _____
Take warm clothes and a blanket. You will need a hat, long trousers and a wool jumper to keep you warm at night. During the day, cover your body, head and face. Clothes protect you from the sun and keep water in your body. You will also need a warm blanket at night. It can get cold very quickly. This drop in temperature can be a shock and make you feel even colder.

E _____
A car is easier to see than a person walking in the desert. You can also use the mirrors from your car to signal to planes and other cars. You can use your car tyres to make a fire. A fire is easy to see. It will help people to find you and keep you warm at night.

F _____
Try to drink some water at least once every hour. You need your water to last as long as possible. Drink only what you need. When you talk, you lose water from your body. Keep your mouth closed and do not talk.

G _____
If you eat, you will get thirsty and drink all of your water more quickly. You can eat a little, but only to stop you feeling very hungry. Eat very small amounts of food and eat very slowly. You can live three weeks with no food, but you can only live three days with no water.

H _____
It is very important to stay out of the sun during the day. Make a hole under your car and lie there. This will keep you cool and help you sleep. Find a warm place to sleep at night. A small place near a tree or a rock will be the warmest. But be careful before you decide where to sleep. Dangerous animals like snakes and scorpions also like to sleep in these places. Look carefully for animals before you lie down.

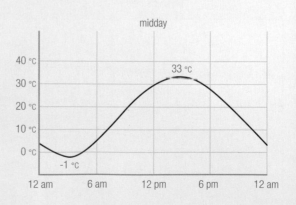

WHILE READING

5 Match the titles (1–5) to the paragraphs (D–H) in the article.

1 Stay out of the sun   _____

2 Drink water   _____

3 Stay cool during the day and warm at night   _____

4 Don't eat too much   _____

5 Stay with your car   _____

READING FOR MAIN IDEAS

UNLOCK ONLINE

6 Look at the graph opposite and read paragraph B. Match the sentence halves.

1	The coldest time is	a	between 2 pm and 4 pm.
2	The average amount of rain in a year	b	is -1 °C.
3	The temperature is 33 °C	c	is 70 mm.
4	The coldest temperature at night	d	at 4 o'clock in the morning.

READING FOR DETAIL

7 Circle the advice that appears in the article.

a Take a hat.

b Don't wear a lot of clothes.

c Try not to drink your water too soon – keep it for later.

d Don't eat quickly.

e Sleep in your car during the day.

f Be careful not to lie down on snakes and scorpions.

READING BETWEEN THE LINES

8 Where might you find an article like this?

a the front page of a newspaper

b a travel magazine

c a geography textbook

RECOGNIZING TEXT TYPE

DISCUSSION

9 Look at the list below. Which things would you like most if you were alone in the desert? Choose the three most important things.

a	a blanket	d	a radio
b	a mirror	e	a map
c	25 litres of water	f	a hat

10 Work with a partner. Compare your answers and explain your choices.

LANGUAGE DEVELOPMENT

COLLOCATIONS WITH *TEMPERATURE*

A

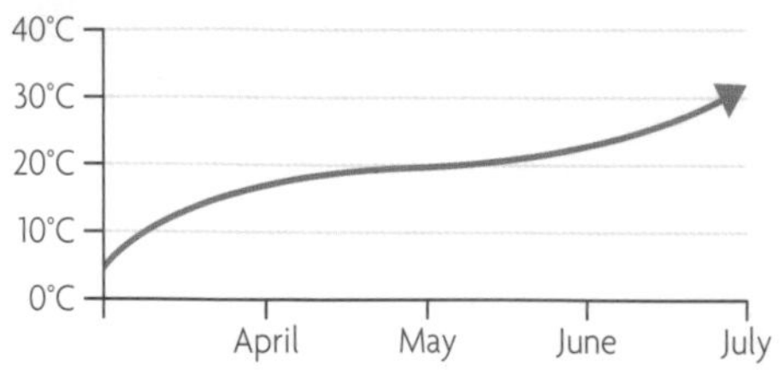

B

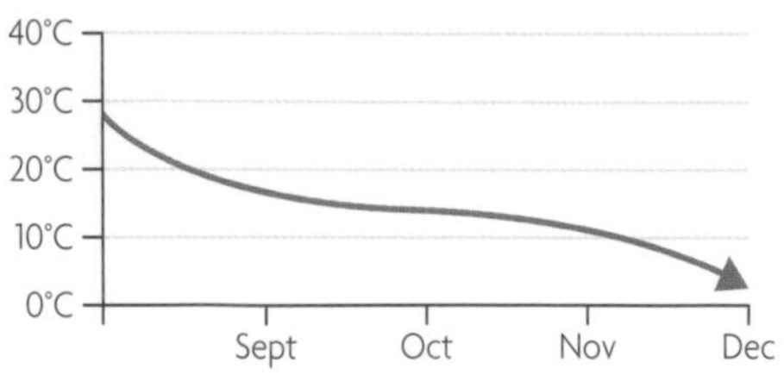

UNLOCK ONLINE

1 Look at the graphs. Circle the correct word to complete the sentences about the graphs.

1 In July, there are *high / low* temperatures.
2 In December, there are *high / low* temperatures.
3 The *maximum / minimum* temperature in July is 32 °C.
4 The *maximum / minimum* temperature in December is 1 °C.

DESCRIBING A GRAPH

We use certain words and phrases to talk about graphs. We use the verbs *rise, drop, fall* and *reach* and the nouns *increase* and *decrease* to describe changes on a graph.

2 Match the sentences to the correct graph (A or B).

1 The graph shows an **increase** in temperature. ______
2 The graph shows a **decrease** in temperature. ______

3 Match the sentences to the correct graph (A or B).

1 The temperature **rises** to 30 °C. ______
2 The temperature **drops** to 1 °C. ______
3 The temperature **falls** to 1 °C. ______
4 The temperature **reaches** 30 °C. ______

4 Write the bold words in Exercise 3 in the gaps to complete the statements.

1 We use ____________ and ____________ to talk about an increase in temperature.
2 We use ____________ and ____________ to talk about a decrease in temperature.

5 Look at the graphs below. Circle the correct word to complete the sentence.

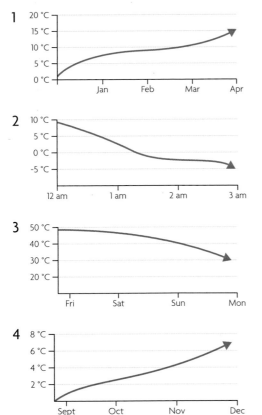

1

a The graph shows *an increase / a decrease* in temperature.

b In April, the temperature *reaches / falls to* 16 °C.

2

a The graph shows *an increase / a decrease* in temperature.

b At 3 o'clock, the temperature *drops / rises to* about -5 °C.

3

a The graph shows *an increase / a decrease* in temperature.

b On Monday, the temperature *reaches / falls to* 30 °C.

4

a The graph shows *an increase / a decrease* in temperature.

b In December, the temperature *rises / falls to* 7 °C.

CRITICAL THINKING

At the end of this unit, you will write sentences to describe a graph. Look at this unit's Writing task in the box below.

> Describe a graph.

Analyze a graph

We use graphs to show numbers or *data*. When we look at a graph, we can see the most interesting information quickly and easily. When we write about graphs, we choose the most interesting information to write about. When we do this, we often look at the highest and lowest numbers.

1 Look at the two graphs. What country do they show information for?

A Rainfall in millimetres over a year in Samarkand, Uzbekistan

B Temperature in degrees centigrade over a year in Samarkand, Uzbekistan

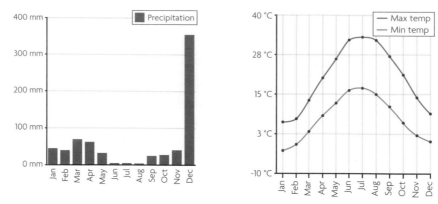

2 Circle the correct words to complete the sentences (1–5).

1 Graph A shows *temperature in degrees centigrade / rainfall in millimetres / the number of hurricanes*.

2 Graph B shows *temperature in degrees centigrade / rainfall in millimetres / the number of hurricanes*.

3 The graphs show data for a period of *one day / one month / one year*.

4 Graph A is *a line graph / a bar graph*.

5 Graph B is *a line graph / a bar graph*.

3 Write an appropriate number for each month in the table below using the information from the graphs.

	J	F	M	A	M	J	J	A	S	O	N	D
temperature												
rainfall												

4 Look at the table in Exercise 3 and the graphs in Exercise 1. Circle the most important information in the table.

5 Look at the table and the graphs again and answer the questions below.

1 Which is the month with the highest temperature? _____

2 Which is the month with the lowest temperature? _____

3 Which is the month with the most rain? _____

4 Which is the month with the least rain? _____

5 Is there anything else in the graph that is interesting? _____

6 Look at the table again and answer the questions below.

1 What extreme weather do you think this place might have?

2 What problems might this cause for the people who live there?

UNLOCK READING AND WRITING SKILLS 2

WRITING

GRAMMAR FOR WRITING

EXPLANATION

Comparative and superlative adjectives

We use *comparative adjective + than* to compare people, things, actions and events.

> The Sahara desert is **hotter than** Cairo.

We use *the + superlative adjective* to say how something is number one in a group.

> The Sahara desert is **the hottest** place in Egypt.

We use *as + adjective + as* to say that people or things are equal.

> Cairo is **as hot as** Dubai

1 Look at the examples in the table below. Put the rules (a–e) in the correct place (1–5) in the table below.

UNLOCK ONLINE

a Some comparatives and superlatives are irregular.
b With an adjective that has one syllable, we add *-er* or *the -est*.
c With an adjective that has two or more syllables, we write *more* or *the most* before the adjective.
d With an adjective that has two syllables and ends in *-y*, we delete the *-y* and add *-ier* or *the -iest*.
e With an adjective that has one vowel and one consonant, we double the consonant and add *-er* or *the -est*.

adjective	comparative	superlative	rule
cold	colder than	the coldest	1 _____
big	bigger than	the biggest	2 _____
easy	easier than	the easiest	3 _____
extreme	more extreme than	the most extreme	4 _____
bad good low	worse than better than lower than	the worst the best the lowest	5 _____

2 Look at the fact files for Cuba and Iceland. In the sentences (1–7) below, use the word in brackets to make a comparative or superlative adjective and write it in the gap.

FACT FILE CUBA

- Maximum temperature: 32 °C
- Minimum temperature: 18 °C
- Average rainfall: 173 mm
- Average sunshine: 7.5 hours a day

FACT FILE ICELAND

- Maximum temperature: 14 °C
- Minimum temperature: -2 °C
- Average rainfall: 94 mm
- Average sunshine: 3.4 hours a day

1 Cuba has a _____ maximum temperature than Iceland. (high)
2 Iceland is _____ than Cuba. (cold)
3 Iceland has the _____ temperature. (low)
4 Cuba is _____ than Iceland. (wet)
5 Iceland is _____ than Cuba. (dry)
6 Cuba is the _____ country. (rainy)
7 Iceland is not as _____ as Cuba. (sunny)

ACADEMIC WRITING SKILLS

EXPLANATION

Introductory sentences for descriptive paragraphs about a graph

When we write about a graph, we use the phrase *the graph shows* to describe the topic of the graph.

The graph shows the temperature in degrees centigrade over a day in the Sahara desert.

Notice how we use the following order:

The graph shows + what is measured + time period + place.

1 Complete the introductory sentences about the graphs in the Critical thinking section (page 116).

1 Graph A shows the _____ in millimetres over one _____ in _____ .

2 Graph B shows the _____ in degrees centigrade over one _____ in _____ .

Using data to support main ideas

When we write about graphs, we use numbers, or *data*, to support our main ideas.

2 In the pairs of sentences below, underline the main idea. Circle the data.

   1 The hottest time is between 2 pm and 4 pm. Temperatures rise to 33 °C.

   2 The coldest time is at 4 am. Temperatures fall to -1 °C.

3 Match the sentence halves to complete the statements.

   1 The main idea   **a** describes a feature or trend from the graph.

   2 The data   **b** is a number from the graph to illustrate the trend.

4 Match the main ideas (1–4) to the data (a–d).

1 Princetown is as rainy as Chesterton.	**a** There are 8.7 hours of sunshine in July and 8 hours of sunshine in August.
2 The hottest month is March.	**b** Temperatures reach 37 °C.
3 July is sunnier than August.	**c** Both towns have an average rainfall of 110 mm.
4 The coldest month is December.	**d** Temperatures fall to -7 °C.

WRITING TASK

> Describe a graph.

UNLOCK ONLINE

1 Look at the graphs on page 116 again. Write a topic sentence about each graph.

   A _____

   B _____

PLAN

2 Choose the two most interesting facts about temperature on each graph. Write a sentence about each fact. Use data to support the statements.

   A 1 _____

      2 _____

   B 1 _____

      2 _____

3 Choose the two most interesting facts about rainfall on each graph. Write a sentence about each fact. Use data to support the statements.

   A 1 _____

      2 _____

   B 1 _____

      2 _____

4 Write a first draft of your sentences.

5 Use the task checklist to review your sentences for content and structure.

TASK CHECKLIST	✔
Have you written an introductory sentence about the graph?	
Have you written five sentences to describe the graph?	
Have you written a topic sentence about the graph?	
Have you used data to support the main ideas?	

6 Make any necessary changes to your sentences.

7 Now use the language checklist to edit your sentences for language errors which are common to A2 learners.

LANGUAGE CHECKLIST	✔
Have you used the correct collocations with *temperature*?	
Have you used the correct vocabulary to describe the graph?	
Have you used comparative and superlative adjectives correctly?	

8 Make any necessary changes to your sentences.

OBJECTIVES REVIEW

9 Check your objectives.

I can ...

watch and understand a
video about people who
follow storms.

very well   not very well

use knowledge to
predict content.

very well   not very well

write a topic sentence to
describe a graph and use
data to support ideas.

very well   not very well

write sentences to
describe a graph.

very well   not very well

WORDLIST

UNIT VOCABULARY			
decrease (n)	shock (n)	decide (v)	careful (adj)
desert (n)	signal (v)	destroy (v)	dangerous (adj)
expert (n)	storm (n)	drop (v)	high (adj)
flood (n)	temperature (n)	fall (v)	huge (adj)
increase (n)	thunder (n)	last (v)	low (adj)
jumper (n)	tornado (n)	predict (v)	maximum (adj)
lightning (n)	tyre (n)	protect (v)	minimum (adj)
mirror (n)	cause (v)	rise (n)	
rainfall (n)	cover (v)	survive (v)	
season (n)	damage (v)	almost (adv)	

LEARNING OBJECTIVES

Watch and listen	Watch and understand a video about sports and competition
Reading skills	Scan for key words to predict content
Academic writing skills	Organize a paragraph in time order and use linkers to show the order
Writing task	Write a process paragraph

UNLOCK YOUR KNOWLEDGE

Work with a partner. Discuss the questions below.

1 Do you play any sports? Why / Why not?
2 Do you like watching sports? If so, which sports do you enjoy watching?
3 Do you have a favourite team or player?
4 Why do you think people like watching sport?
5 Do you think there is too much or too little sport on TV?

WATCH AND LISTEN

PREPARING TO WATCH

UNDERSTANDING KEY VOCABULARY

1 Match the words (1–7) to their definitions (a–g).

1	a championship	**a**	practising to learn or improve a new skill
2	training	**b**	a very important competition to find the best person
3	a go-kart	**c**	something that you want to do
4	a licence	**d**	a small car used for racing
5	a track	**e**	a road or path used for races or sports events
6	a dream	**f**	official permission to do something
7	overtake	**g**	when one car passes another car

PREVIEWING

2 Work in pairs. You are going to watch a video about a race-car driver. Before you watch, read the newspaper headline and discuss the questions below.

> **Marika Diana is first woman to win national championships**

1 How old do you think Marika Diana is?
2 Do you think she's a professional race-car driver?
3 What country do you think she lives in?
4 Do you think the sport is popular in her country?

3 ▶ Watch the video and check your answers.

WHILE WATCHING

UNDERSTANDING MAIN IDEAS

4 ▶ Watch again. Circle the correct words to complete the sentences.

1 Marika *does / doesn't* have a normal driver's licence.
2 Marika started racing *with her parents / when she was young.*
3 She trains every week in *cars / go-karts.*
4 She *needs / doesn't need* to finish first, second or third in this race.
5 Marika *wins / doesn't win* the race.

5 ▶ Watch again. Write a number from the video in each gap to complete the sentences.

1 Marika is _____ years old now.
2 She started racing when she was _____ years old.
3 Many Formula _____ champions drove go-karts when they were young.
4 Motor sports started over _____ years ago.
5 The top speed of a race car is _____ kilometres per hour.
6 In the car, Marika is only _____ centimetres above the ground.
7 She won each of the _____ last races.
8 At the end of the race, Marika finishes in _____nd place.
9 Marika is the _____st woman to win this race in Italy.

6 The video says that Marika *does not give up*. What does this mean? Circle the two best definitions. Compare your answers with your partner.

1 She does not give something to other drivers.
2 She does not stop following her dream.
3 She does not drive faster in the race.
4 She does not stop trying her best.

7 Answer the questions below. Compare your answers with a partner.

1 What do you think Marika means whens she says *It's something that comes from inside*? _____
2 Why does the narrator in the video say that it is a great day for Marika? _____

DISCUSSION

8 Work with a partner. Discuss the questions below.

1 What sports are popular in your country?
2 Who are the most famous sportsmen and sportswomen in your country?
3 Are there any sports in your country that are played mainly by men or mainly by women?
4 Is it important to love the sport you do? Why / Why not?

PREPARING TO READ

UNDERSTANDING KEY VOCABULARY

1 Match the words (1–7) to their definitions (a–g).

1 major	**a** a running race of about 42.2 kilometres
2 take place	**b** a sport in which two people hit each other while wearing big, leather gloves
3 a race	
4 a marathon	**c** important or big
5 ancient	**d** from a very, very long time ago
6 boxing	**e** a part of a competition, e.g. first, second, third
7 a round	**f** a competition in which people try to be the fastest and finish first
	g happen

SCANNING TO PREDICT CONTENT

2 Look at the words in bold in paragraph A of the text opposite and answer the questions below.

1 What is the main topic of the text?
   a unusual competitions
   b unusual sports
   c popular sports

2 Where do the events in the text happen?
   a in one country
   b around the world
   c in a city

3 Look at the words in bold again. What types of words are they?
   a verbs
   b adjectives
   c articles
   d nouns
   e prepositions

Scanning to predict content

Before we read a text, we often scan for *key words*. Key words are usually nouns, verbs and adjectives. The key words tell us what the text is going to be about.

3 Read the text and check your answers.

SPORTING NEWS.com

Five strange sports
our most unusual sports from around the world

A Every **country** has a national **sport** and most major **sports** are now played across the **world**. Most people have heard of **sports** like football, basketball, cricket and golf. However, in most **countries**, people also play **unusual sports**, with **strange** and interesting rules. Here are our top five **unusual sports** from around the planet.

B _____

This race takes place in Wales. It is called a marathon, but it is actually 35.4 km, not 42.2 km like a usual marathon. People race against horses across the hills and mountains. It started in 1981, but a human did not win until 2004.

C _____

Every year in Singapore, thousands of people come to watch the dragon boat race. A dragon boat is a traditional Chinese boat with a painted dragon's head on one end. There are 22 people in each boat and they race in the water. Dragon boat racing is also popular in China, Malaysia and Indonesia.

D _____

In this sport, people compete to throw a large piece of wood called a caber as far as they can. The caber toss is an ancient Scottish sport. The caber has no official size or shape, but it is usually the size of a small tree.

E _____

You need both strength and intelligence to be a good chess boxer. Players play a round of chess, followed by a round of boxing. There are eleven rounds in total. Chess boxing was invented in 1992 by an English comic book writer. The sport is most popular in England and Germany.

F _____

In Turkey, camel wrestling* is a very old sport. The largest camel wrestling competition takes place in Ephesus every year and thousands of people come. In the sport, two male camels wrestle each other. Sometimes the camels do not want to fight and they run through the crowds, which can be dangerous.

*wrestling = fighting

SKIMMING

UNLOCK ONLINE

READING FOR
DETAIL

RECOGNIZING
TEXT TYPE

WHILE READING

4 Skim the text (p. 127). Match the paragraph titles (1–5) to the paragraphs (B–F).

1 Chess boxing   _____
2 Dragon boat racing   _____
3 Camel wrestling   _____
4 Caber toss   _____
5 Man vs. horse marathon _____

5 Write the names of the countries in which each sport is popular.

1 Chess boxing _____
2 Dragon boat race _____
3 Camel wrestling _____
4 Caber toss _____
5 Man vs. horse marathon _____

6 Read the text again and look at the sentences below. There is one mistake in each sentence. Correct the false information.

1 The man vs. horse marathon is 42.2 kilometres.
2 The man vs. horse marathon began in 1991.
3 A dragon boat has a dragon's tail painted on it.
4 There are 25 people in each dragon boat team.
5 A caber is a large piece of metal.
6 A caber is usually the size of a large tree.
7 There are 2 stages in a chess boxing competition.
8 Chess boxing was invented by a journalist.
9 The Ephesus camel wrestling competition happens twice a year.
10 In camel wrestling, two female camels fight each other.

READING BETWEEN THE LINES

7 What kind of person is this text for?

a someone who is interested in different sports
b someone who wants to learn how to play a new sport

8 Where do you think you might see this text?

a in a newspaper or magazine
b on a website

9 What do you think the text is?

a an advertisement
b an article

DISCUSSION

10 Work with a partner. Discuss the questions below.

   1 What are the advantages of playing sport?

   2 Why do countries spend large amounts of money to organize sports events like the Olympic Games?

READING 2

PREPARING TO READ

1 Before you read, look at the text on page 130. What type of text is it?

PREVIEWING

2 Look at the photographs and read the title of the text. What do you think the topic of the text will be?

3 Read the text and check your answers.

WHILE READING

4 Read the text again and circle the correct words to complete the sentences below.

READING FOR MAIN IDEAS

UNLOCK
ONLINE

   1 Tough man is a very *easy / difficult* competition.

   2 The event takes place when it is very *hot / cold*.

   3 People from many different *countries / cities* take part.

   4 Every year people *get hurt / leave early*.

   5 Participants have to be very *clever / strong* to do the event.

   6 People do the competition because it is *unusual / famous*.

   7 The competition is *different / the same* every year.

5 Look at the diagram of the course on page 130. Match the different parts of the competition (1–6) to the sentences (a–f) from the final paragraph of the text.

   1 Mud run

   2 Nets

   3 High dive and swim

   4 Field of fire

   5 Water tunnel

   6 Nettles

   a Participants must crawl through a long tunnel.

   b The runners run across a field and jump over small bonfires.

   c The runners run 2 km through nettles.

   d Participants run for 1 km along a muddy road.

   e The runners jump off a high platform into a lake and swim for 1 km.

   f They crawl under low nets on the ground.

TOUGH MAN:
a race to the limit

What is Tough Man?

Every January, more than 3,000 people take part in one of the most difficult races on Earth: the Tough Man competition in the UK. Participants run, swim and climb around the 15 km course. But this is no normal race. These runners have to crawl through tunnels, run across a field of nettles and jump over fire. What's more, the competition takes place in January, so temperatures are freezing – sometimes as low as -6 °C. People travel from all over the world to take part, with participants from South Africa, Australia and China.

Why do people take part?

The competition is quite dangerous and every year there are accidents. Injuries like broken bones and cuts are quite common. The race is very hard: one-third of participants do not finish it. Runners have to be very fit and healthy and most people train all year to prepare for the event. It is also the only race like it in the world. There are similar events, but this was the first one in the world. Many people do the competition because it is so famous. Every year the organizers change the event and add new things. This means that the competition stays exciting and challenging, so people go back year after year.

The course

The diagram shows the Tough Man course. First, participants run for 1 km along a muddy road. Next, they crawl under low nets on the ground. After the nets, the runners jump off a high platform into a lake and swim for 1 km. Then, they reach the field of fire. Here, the runners run across a field and jump over small bonfires. Next, participants must crawl through a long tunnel. The tunnel is partly under water. Finally, the runners run 2 km through nettles before they reach the finish line.

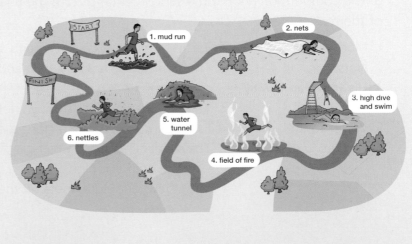

6 Answer the questions below.

   1 Where does the Tough Man competition take place? _____
   2 When does the Tough Man competition take place? _____
   3 How long is the course? _____
   4 How long do people train for the competition? _____
   5 Why do people go back to the competition every year? _____

7 Underline the words (1–4) in the first paragraph of the text opposite. Match the words to their synonyms (a–e). One word has two synonyms.

1 competition   **a** runners
2 participants   **b** participate
3 take part   **c** event
4 course   **d** track
       e race

READING BETWEEN THE LINES

8 The text says that participants have to *run through nettles*. Look at the photograph and the text. What is a nettle?

a a plant
b an animal

9 Why do you think running through nettles is difficult?

a because nettles hurt you
b because nettles smell horrible

DISCUSSION

10 Work with a partner. Discuss the questions below.

   1 Do you know any events like the Tough Man competition?
   2 Why do people keep fit in their free time?
   3 Should people be allowed to do dangerous sports like horseriding and skiing?

⊙ LANGUAGE DEVELOPMENT

Prepositions of movement

We use *prepositions of movement* to describe where somebody or something is going. We use prepositions of movement to give directions.

Walk **past** the shop and **across** the road.

UNLOCK
ONLINE

1 Match the descriptions (1–7) to the pictures (a–g).

1 past a building

2 through a tunnel

3 across a lake

4 around the track

5 along the road

6 over a bridge

7 under the bridge

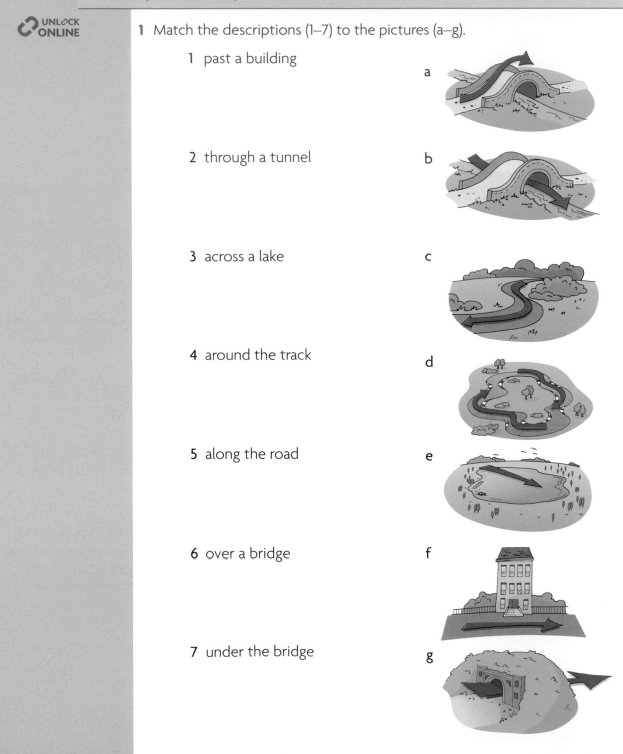

a

b

c

d

e

f

g

2 Look at the map. Write prepositions from Exercise 1 in the gaps to complete the paragraph below. You might need to use some prepositions more than once.

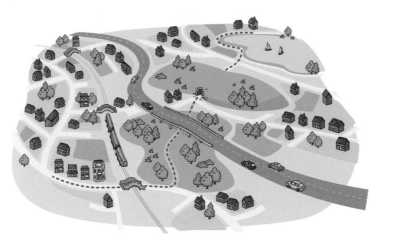

> It is easy to get to my house. First, walk ⁽¹⁾_____ the High Street. Go ⁽²⁾_____ the bank and ⁽³⁾_____ the bridge. Then, walk ⁽⁴⁾_____ the park and ⁽⁵⁾_____ the motorway bridge. Go ⁽⁶⁾_____ the tunnel – be careful of cars – and walk ⁽⁷⁾_____ the road. Walk ⁽⁸⁾_____ the lake, and my house is at the end of the road.

CRITICAL THINKING

At the end of this unit, you will write a process paragraph. Look at this unit's Writing task in the box below.

> Write a process paragraph to describe the Sydney triathlon.

Analyzing a diagram

In academic writing, we often have to write about diagrams. It is important to analyze the information in the diagram carefully before you write. It is sometimes important to understand the order of the events in the diagram and the effect that different events have on each other.

1 Look at the diagram of the triathlon course in Sydney below. Write the words from the box in the gaps (1–6) to label the diagram.

central library   bridge   tunnel   cycle route   run route   swim route

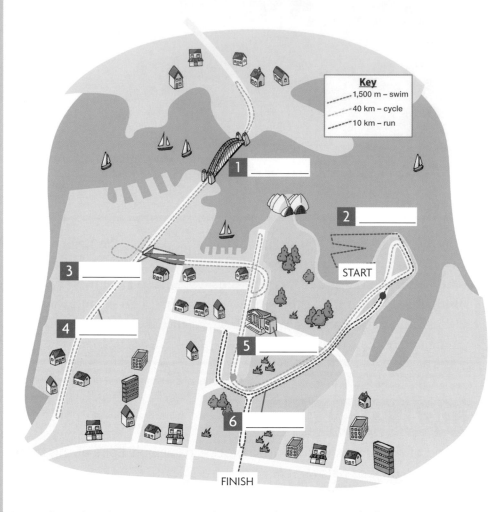

Key
1,500 m – swim
40 km – cycle
10 km – run

1 _____
2 _____
3 _____
4 _____
5 _____
6 _____

START

FINISH

2 Look at the diagram again and answer the questions below.

1 How far do the participants have to run?   _____
2 How far do the participants have to swim?   _____
3 How far do the participants have to cycle?   _____

3 Look at the diagram again. What do the competitors in the triathlon have to do? Write prepositions in the gaps to complete the phrases below.

a cycle _____ the bridge
b cycle _____ the tunnel
c run _____ the road
d swim _____ the lake   1
e run _____ central library

4 Number the parts of the race (a–e) in Exercise 3 to show the correct order of the triathlon. The first one has been done for you.

WRITING

GRAMMAR FOR WRITING

Subject and verb agreement

In a sentence, we have to use the correct form of the verb to match the subject.

We use the *singular* form of the verb with singular subjects.

The race **begins** at 3 pm.
Last year's winner **is** at the start of the race.

We use the *plural* form of the verb with plural subjects.

The footballers **play** three times a week.
Football and tennis **are** popular sports.

UNL♥CK ONLINE

1 Look at the sentences below. Underline the subject and circle the verb.

　1 They play sports every day.
　2 We watch the World Cup finals at home.
　3 She runs across the field.
　4 It is a popular sport in Asia.
　5 You run over the bridge.
　6 I love motor racing.

2 Circle the correct form of the verb in the sentences below.

　1 She *is / am* a tennis player.
　2 He *swim / swims* every day.
　3 They *walks / walk* over the bridge.
　4 The fastest runner *win / wins* the trophy.
　5 Oleg and I *practise / practises* hockey after school.
　6 Skiing *are / is* a winter sport.

3 Write the correct form of the verb in brackets in the gaps to complete the sentences below.

　1 I _____ to practise every day. (try)
　2 The team captain _____ the trophy. (carry)
　3 Dragon boat racing _____ an unusual sport. (be)
　4 My friends and I _____ sport on TV. (watch)
　5 Footballers often _____ penalty goals. (miss)
　6 He _____ (want) to be a Formula One driver.
　7 The teams and the referee _____ (run) onto the field.
　8 Cricket and rugby _____ (be) popular sports in the UK.
　9 The players _____ (catch) the ball.

ACADEMIC WRITING SKILLS

EXPLANATION

Ordering events in a process

When we write about a process, we usually write about events in the order that they happen. We use *linkers* to organize our ideas and show the order in our writing.

We use the linkers *first, second, third* and *finally* to show the order that events happen in a process. We also use *next, then* and *after that* to show order.

First, the participants run 10 km. **Second,** they swim across the river. Participants run 10 km. **Then,** they swim across the river.

We use these linkers at the beginning of a sentence, followed by a comma.

1 Match the sentences (1–4) to the pictures (a–d).

1 The weightlifter lifts the weight onto his shoulders.   _____
2 The weightlifter drops the weight to the ground.   _____
3 The weightlifter lifts the weight above his head.   _____
4 The weightlifter holds the weight above his head for as long as he can.   _____

a   b

c   d

2 Rewrite the sentences in Exercise 1 in the correct order using *first, second, third* and *finally*.

1 _____
2 _____
3 _____
4 _____

3 Rewrite the paragraph below with the linkers from the box to show the order of the events. Remember to use commas. More than one answer is possible.

next   then   after that

> The players walk onto the court. They pick up their racquets. One player hits the ball over the net. The other player hits the ball back.

_____

_____

4 Work with a partner. Compare and discuss your answers.

ELIMINATING IRRELEVANCIES

When we do a writing task, it is important to write only about relevant information. Before we write, we need to decide what information is important and only write about information that is directly relevant to the question. After we write, it is a good idea to check for any information that is not important and delete it.

5 Read the title of the writing task and the paragraph below. Cross out the information in the paragraph that is not important.

> Write a process paragraph to describe how to do the high jump.
>
> The high jump is an Olympic sport that is practised in many countries. ~~Athletes competed in over 30 venues during the 2012 London Olympic Games.~~ First, the high jumper runs towards the bar. It is important to run very fast. High jump is the most popular sport in Russia. Second, the high jumper jumps. I was on the high jump team at school. The high jumper must jump from the right foot and keep their arms close to their sides. Next, the high jumper twists their body so their back is to the bar. They must lift their head and feet and keep them high above the bar. The high jump is a really interesting sport. After that, the high jumper lands. They must be careful to land safely on the mat. Javier Sotomayor is the current high jump world champion. Finally, the high jumper stands up, takes a bow and leaves the mat.

6 Work with a partner. Compare and discuss your answers.

WRITING TASK

Write a process paragraph to describe the Sydney triathlon.

1 Use your notes from the Critical thinking section (page 134) to complete the paragraph planner below. Write any general information in column A. Put the events in the triathlon in the correct order in column B.

A	B
	1
	2
	3
	4
	5

2 Start your paragraph by writing about the general information in the diagram. This is the introduction.

3 Write about the events in the triathlon in the correct order and use linkers to show the time order. This is the main body.

4 Use the task checklist to review your paragraph for content and structure.

TASK CHECKLIST	✔
Have you written about the general information and the events in the triathlon?	
Have you put the events in the correct order?	
Have you used linkers to show the order of the events clearly?	
Have you eliminated any irrelevant information?	

5 Make any necessary changes to your paragraph.

6 Now use the language checklist to edit your paragraph for language errors which are common to A2 learners.

LANGUAGE CHECKLIST	✔
Have you used the correct prepositions of movement?	
Have you used subject and verb agreement correctly?	

7 Make any necessary changes to your paragraph.

OBJECTIVES REVIEW

8 Check your objectives.

I can ...

watch and understand a
video about sports and   very   not very
competition.   well   well

scan for key words to
predict content.   very   not very
                             well   well

organize a paragraph in
time order and use linkers   very   not very
to show the order.   well   well

write a process paragraph.
                             very   not very
                             well   well

WORDLIST

UNIT VOCABULARY		
boxing (n)	course (n)	take place (v)
championship (n)	marathon (n)	ancient (adj)
competitor (n)	race (n)	major (adj)
dream (n)	round (n)	finally (adv)
competition (n)	team (n)	first (adv)

LEARNING OBJECTIVES

Watch and listen	Watch and understand a video about business success
Reading skills	Work out meaning from context
Academic writing skills	Add detail to main facts
Writing task	Write a narrative paragraph

UNL⌀CK YOUR KNOWLEDGE

1 Discuss the questions below.
   1 An entrepreneur is a person who starts a new business.
     Do you know the names of the famous entrepreneurs in the
     photographs?
   2 Do you know the names of the companies they started?
   3 Do you know the names of any other famous entrepreneurs
     from your country?

2 Look at the adjectives in the box. Which of these are important
  qualities for an entrepreneur to have?

   careful   clever   friendly   good with computers   polite
   good with money   happy   hardworking   kind   funny

3 Do you think you would be a good entrepreneur?

WATCH AND LISTEN

PREPARING TO WATCH

1 Before you watch, read the sentence from the video and look at the underlined word.

> To be a <u>success</u>, companies must change, or adapt, to the world around them.

1 Circle the correct meaning of *success*.
  a something that fails or that loses money
  b something that has a good result or that is very popular

2 Write *V* (verb), *N* (noun) and *A* (adjective) next to the words (a–c) below.
  a success _____
  b successful _____
  c succeed _____

2 Match the words (1–10) to their definitions (a–j).

1	a fashion designer	**a**	a design of lines, shapes and colours
2	improve	**b**	liked by many people
3	a mathematician	**c**	involving competition
4	a pattern	**d**	a chance to do something good
5	an industry	**e**	a picture or short film that is designed to persuade people to buy something
6	a company	**f**	all the companies that do one kind of business
7	popular	**g**	a person who studies or teaches maths
8	competitive	**h**	a person who draws and plans how to make clothes
9	an advertisement	**i**	get better or make something better
10	an opportunity	**j**	an organization that sells products or services

3 You are going to watch a video about three companies: EA Games, Ferrari, and Jhane Barnes.

  1 Do you know any of the companies?

  2 What does each company do?

4 ▶ Watch the video and check your answers.

WHILE WATCHING

5 ▶ Watch again. Circle the main ideas that are discussed in the video.

  1 Change is important for business success.

  2 Big businesses are more likely to succeed than small businesses.

  3 Successful businesses adapt to new technology.

  4 Most new businesses fail in the first year.

  5 EA Games, Ferrari, and Jhane Barnes have all adapted to change.

6 ▶ Watch again. Write true (T) or false (F) next to the statements below.

  1 The video game industry changes quite slowly. _____

  2 The video game *Pong* was created in 1962. _____

  3 Making cars for Formula One is very competitive. _____

  4 Ferrari use technology from their Formula One cars in their road cars. _____

  5 Ferrari's road cars sell for millions of pounds. _____

  6 Ferrari make advertisements. _____

  7 Jhane Barnes met Bill Jones in the 1980s. _____

  8 Bill Jones creates patterns on a computer. _____

  9 Jhane Barnes and Bill Jones work together to make clothes. _____

DISCUSSION

7 Work with a partner. Discuss the questions below.

  1 Which are the most successful companies in your country?

  2 Why are some companies more successful than others?

  3 Should governments help companies which are not successful?

READING 1

PREPARING TO READ

SCANNING TO
PREDICT CONTENT

1 Before you read, look at the text opposite quickly. What kind of text is it?

   a an encyclopaedia entry

   b an online quiz

   c a newspaper article

2 What question (a–c) is the best description of the topic of the text?

   a What kind of job would suit you?

   b Could you be an entrepreneur?

   c What makes a good businessperson?

3 Read the text and check your answers.

WHILE READING

READING FOR
MAIN IDEAS

4 Read the text again. Correct the mistakes in the paragraph below using words from the text.

UNL**⌀**CK
ONLINE

> There are <u>three</u> main kinds of work – work with animals, work
> with information, work with machines and work with ideas.
> The questionnaire helps you to find out about the kind of people
> you might like. After the questionnaire, you read the advice to find
> universities you may like.

READING FOR
DETAIL

5 Do the quiz in the text. Circle your answers and count the letters you chose. Read the advice about jobs for you.

6 Do you agree or disagree with the advice?

READING BETWEEN THE LINES

WORKING OUT
MEANING

7 Find the words from the box below in the text opposite and underline them.

occupations   colleagues   advice   customers

Are you ready for the
world of work?

Do you know what kind of job you want? Before you decide, think about the different types of jobs that people do. There are four main types of jobs:

1 jobs with people
2 jobs with information
3 jobs with things
4 jobs with ideas

What kind of work would be best for you? Take our quiz and find out about the kind of work you would enjoy. For each question, click on the best answer for you: a, b, c or d.

Check your results and read the advice below to find occupations you would like.

---

1 What do you like to do in the evenings?
- a meet friends or go to a party
- b stay at home and surf the internet
- c play sport or practise a hobby
- d go to the cinema

2 Which parts of the newspaper do you look at first?
- a advice column or letters to the editor
- b news
- c sports
- d TV, music, books and art

3 What do you like to do at a party?
- a meet new people
- b discuss the latest news
- c help with the food and drink
- d sing songs and tell jokes

4 What do you prefer to do on a day off?
- a have coffee with friends
- b tidy your books and cupboards
- c work in the garden, or clean your house
- d write poetry, make music or draw pictures

Mostly 'a' answers:
You are friendly, kind and interested in other people. You would enjoy a job working with children or customers in a shop, or in a team with colleagues. Possible jobs are: teacher, waiter, police officer.

Mostly 'b' answers:
You are tidy, organized and you like learning new things. You would enjoy a job working with information. Possible jobs are: university lecturer, computer programmer, librarian.

Mostly 'c' answers:
You are practical, good at sports and you like working with your hands. You would enjoy a job working with things. Possible jobs are: builder, engineer, farmer.

Mostly 'd' answers:
You are creative, good at music and art, and you like books. You would enjoy a job working with ideas. Possible jobs are: artist, writer, singer.

8 Read the text around the underlined words and circle the best definition for each word.

1 advice (n)
   a suggestions about what you think someone should do
   b instructions to tell someone exactly what to do
2 an occupation (n)
   a a hobby
   b a job
3 a customer (n)
   a a type of computer programme
   b a person that buys things from a shop or business
4 a colleague (n)
   a a person you work with
   b a good friend

Working out meaning from context

When we read, we often see words that we do not know. However, it is often possible to understand the meaning of new words in a text from the context (the topic and the other words in the text).

IDENTIFYING THE
AUDIENCE

9 Who would be interested in the quiz? Circle the correct answer. More than one answer is possible.

a a new worker in a company
b a new graduate from university
c a high school student

DISCUSSION

10 Work with a partner. Discuss the questions below.

1 What would be your perfect job?
2 What type of job would you hate?

READING 2

PREPARING TO READ

1 Before you read, write the words from the box in the gaps to complete the definitions.

UNDERSTANDING KEY VOCABULARY

> knit   handmade   wool   goal   introduce   expand

1 _____ is the hair from a sheep.
2 Something _____ is made by a person, not a machine.
3 When you _____ , you make clothes out of wool by hand.
4 _____ means gets bigger.
5 A _____ is something you want to do.
6 When you _____ something, you show something new to people.

2 Scan paragraph A of the article on page 149. Underline two synonyms for the word *grandmother*.

3 Circle the words from Exercise 1 in the article and read the title. What do you think the article is about?

SCANNING TO PREDICT CONTENT

4 Read the article and check your answers.

WHILE READING

5 Read the article again. Choose the best heading (A–C) for each paragraph.

READING FOR MAIN IDEAS

1 Why Golden Hook is great   A / B / C
2 Special hats made just for you   A / B / C
3 The story of Golden Hook   A / B / C

UNLOCK ONLINE

6 Read the article again and circle the correct answers to the questions.

1 What does the company make?
   a clothes
   b websites
2 Where does the company make the products?
   a in a factory
   b in people's homes
3 How does the company make the products?
   a by hand
   b with machines
4 Who makes things in the company?
   a young men
   b older women

7 Read the article again and write true (T) or false (F) next to the statements below.

   1 Twenty women work for Golden Hook.   _____
   2 You can only buy Golden Hook hats in Paris, London,
      New York and Tokyo.   _____
   3 All Golden Hook hats are the same colour.   _____
   4 The women love working for Golden Hook.   _____

8 Look at the events in the Golden Hook business story in the table below.

   1 In column A, number the events (1–4) in the order that they happened.
   2 In column B, write the year of each event.

	A	B
Jérémy had the idea for Golden Hook.		
Jérémy began knitting hats.		
A famous Japanese shop started selling Golden Hook hats.		
The Golden Hook website started.		

READING BETWEEN THE LINES

9 What do you think is the author's opinion of the Golden Hook company? Circle the correct answer.

   a The author thinks it is a good idea.
   b The author thinks it is a bad idea.

10 In which paragraph did you find the answer? _____

DISCUSSION

11 Work with a partner. Discuss the questions below.

   1 Do you think Golden Hook is a good idea? Why / Why not?
   2 Would you like to have your own business? Why / Why not?
   3 If you had your own business, what would it be?

You can choose your grandma!

A Have you heard of Golden Hook? Golden Hook is a group of twenty grannies and a young man with a clever business idea. They make beautiful, handmade, wool hats and sell them all around the world. You don't buy Golden Hook hats in a shop. If you want one, you go to their website and choose the style, size and colours you want. Then you look at photographs and choose a grandma. The granny knits the hat by hand just for you. One week later, you get the hat with a special message from the granny inside. You can see people wearing Golden Hook hats in Paris, London, Tokyo and New York. People love the hats because every hat is different.

B Golden Hook was started in Paris, by Jérémy Emsellem. In 2005, when he was 19, Jérémy began knitting hats for fun. He wore the hats in class, and other students really liked them. Everyone wanted one! Jérémy made hats for 50 students, but he didn't have time to make hats for everyone. Then, in 2007, he visited his old aunt and had an idea. His aunt and her friends were all grandmothers. They didn't have a job and they didn't look after children, so they had lots of time. They were really bored. They were also very good at knitting. Jérémy talked to his aunt's friends. He asked them if they wanted to make his hats. Six of the grandmothers said 'Yes'. In 2008, Jérémy started the Golden Hook company and set up the website. In the first year, they only sold 300 hats, but the company expanded quickly. Soon after, in 2010, Golden Hook employed 20 grannies. Three years later, in 2012, a famous shop introduced the hats to Tokyo – Japanese people loved the grannies' hats. In the future, Jérémy's goal is to have Golden Hook grannies all over the world.

C With Golden Hook, everyone wins. The customers get excellent hats. The grannies get money, and something interesting to do. And Jérémy? Jérémy is 25, and the CEO* of an international company.

          * a CEO (Chief Executive Officer) is the person in charge of a business.

⦿ LANGUAGE DEVELOPMENT

COLLOCATIONS WITH *BUSINESS*

1 The words in the diagram are collocations of *business*. Write *N* next to the nouns and *V* next to the verbs.

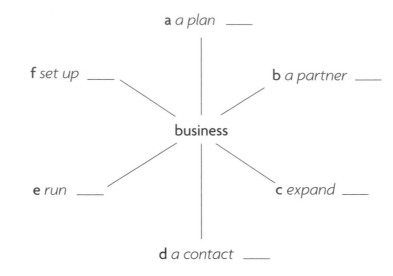

a *a plan* ____

f *set up* ____

b *a partner* ____

business

e *run* ____

c *expand* ____

d *a contact* ____

2 Write words from the diagram in the gaps to complete the definitions (1–6).

1 A **business** _____ is a detailed document describing the future plans of a business.

2 _____ **a business** means to make a business bigger.

3 A **business** _____ is a person who owns a business with you.

4 _____ **a business** means to be in charge of and control a business.

5 _____ **a business** means to start a business.

6 A **business** _____ is a person you know because of your job.

3 Look at the sentences in Exercise 2 again and answer the questions below.

1 Do the verbs go before or after the word *business*?

2 Do the nouns go before or after the word *business*?

BUSINESS VOCABULARY

4 Match the words (1–5) to their definitions (a–e).

1 employ   **a** a type of computer program

2 employee   **b** give someone a job

3 office   **c** a place where people work

4 software   **d** something a business makes to sell

5 product   **e** a worker

5 Write the words from Exercise 4 in the gaps to complete the email below. You may have to use the plural form of some words.

New message

Important information for all ¹_____ of Jenson Co.

I am pleased to tell you that we are moving into a bright new ²_____ this week. We are also getting new ³_____ for our computers. We will have more space, so we can ⁴_____ some more members of staff. I am very confident that these changes will help us sell more of our excellent ⁵_____ .

Best,

James Curry

MD

CRITICAL THINKING

At the end of this unit, you will write a narrative paragraph. Look at this unit's Writing task in the box below.

> Write a narrative paragraph about the business history of Google.

Making inferences

We *make inferences* when we use clues or our own knowledge to work something out. We use logic to make inferences.

1 The spider diagram below shows eight facts (a–h) about Google's business history. Put the events in the order you think they happened (1–8).

ANALYZE

☐ **d** Larry Page and Sergey Brin meet at Stanford University.
_____

☐ **c** Google expands to one billion web pages.
_____

☐ **a** Google Earth is launched.
_____

☐ **e** Google Chrome is launched.
_____

The Google Story

☐ **g** Larry Page and Sergey Brin set up Google.
_____

☐ **f** 'Google' becomes a verb in British and American English dictionaries.
_____

☐ **b** Google employs its first worker, Craig Silverstein.
_____

☐ **h** Google's yearly profit is $37 billion.
_____

2 Listen to your teacher. Write the years from the box below next to the events on the spider diagram (page 151).

1995   1997   1998   2000   2005   2006   2008   2011

Using a timeline to put past events in order

When we write about things that happened in the past, we usually write about them in chronological order. We start with the event that happened first and end with the event that happened last. Timelines are a useful way to organize past events in chronological order.

CREATE

3 Put the events in Google's history in the correct place on the timeline below. Write the dates above the timeline and the events (a–h) below.

1995 ____ ____   ____   ____   ____   ____

d

a Google Earth is launched.
b Google employs its first worker, Craig Silverstein.
c Google expands to one billion web pages.
d Larry Page and Sergey Brin meet at Stanford University.
e Google Chrome is launched.
f 'Google' becomes a verb in British and American English dictionaries.
g Larry Page and Sergey Brin set up Google.
h Google's yearly profit is $37 billion.

WRITING

GRAMMAR FOR WRITING

EXPLANATION

Past and present tenses

We use the *present simple* to talk about events that happen in the present or to talk about a general truth. We use the *past simple* to talk about events that happened in the past.

> Apple technology **is** very intelligent.
> Steve Jobs **was** the co-founder, chairman and CEO of Apple.

1 Circle the verbs in the sentences below. Write *past* next to the verbs in the past simple and *present* next to the verbs in the present simple.

1 Ford is one of the most famous motor companies in the world.
2 Jacques Nasser joined Ford in 1968.
3 Jacques Nasser is the son of Abdo Nasser.
4 On 1st January 1999, Jacques Nasser became president of Ford.
5 In 2000, Ford bought Land Rover.
6 In 2003, Ford celebrated its 100th birthday.

2 Circle the correct form of the verb in the paragraph below.

> The JLX company ¹*sells / sold* food to supermarkets and shops.
> In 2009, Michael Underwood ²*sets up / set up* the business.
> In 2010, the company ³*does / did* very well. In June, Michael
> Underwood ⁴*employs / employed* three new employees. The company
> ⁵*expands / expanded* and ⁶*opens / opened* new offices in Europe. Today, JLX
> ⁷*is / was* a very successful business.

3 Put the words in brackets in the correct form of the past simple or present simple.

1 Nissan _____ (be) a Japanese company.
2 In 1824, John Cadbury _____ (open) the first Cadbury's chocolate shop.
3 Lego _____ (sell) toys.
4 Today, Nestlé _____ (be) the world's biggest food and drinks business.
5 Nokia _____ (start) in 1865.
6 In 1995, Amazon _____ (sell) the first book on Amazon.com.
7 Adidas _____ (make) sports clothes around the world.
8 In 1926, Mercedes-Benz _____ (design) its first car.

EXPLANATION

Clauses with *when*

We use *when* with a clause to describe the date or time that something happened.

*He started the business **when** he was sixteen.*

If we want to make the time of the event more important, we can put the *when* clause first and follow it with a comma.

***When** he was sixteen, he started the business.*

4 Rewrite the sentences below using *when*.

1 She became the CEO. She was 30.

_____

2 They employed six new workers. The business expanded.

_____

3 He left his job. He was 65.

_____

4 The shop closed. The economy crashed.

_____

5 They expanded the company. It was still successful.

_____

ACADEMIC WRITING SKILLS

EXPLANATION

Adding detail

In a narrative paragraph, we add detail to the main facts to make what we write more interesting.

Look at the completed timeline from the Critical thinking section (page 152). Match the details (1–8) below to the main facts in the Google story (a–h) on the timeline.

1 This program is a map that shows 3D pictures of streets around the world. _____

2 They are both students. Larry is 22 and Sergey is 21. _____

3 Craig is a student at Stanford University. _____

4 It is a new web browser to compete with Microsoft's internet Explorer. _____

5 They open their first office in a garage in California. _____

6 This is a big increase in profit. _____

7 It becomes the world's biggest internet search company. _____

8 It is a verb which means 'to look for something on the internet'. _____

WRITING TASK

Write a narrative paragraph about the business history of Google.

UNLOCK ONLINE

PLAN

1 Look at the timeline in the Critical thinking section (page 152). Choose the four main facts that you want to include in your paragraph.

2 Write the main facts in time order in the paragraph planner below. Then write the detail under each main fact in the paragraph planner.

Main fact 1	
Detail	
Main fact 2	
Detail	
Main fact 3	
Detail	
Main fact 4	
Detail	

3 Write a topic sentence that explains what you are going to write about.

4 Write a first draft of your paragraph.

5 Use the task checklist to review your paragraph for content and structure.

TASK CHECKLIST	✔
Have you written about the business history of Google?	
Have you written about the four main facts in time order?	
Have you given the date or time that things happened?	
Have you added detail to the main facts?	

6 Make any necessary changes to your paragraph.

7 Now use the language checklist to edit your paragraph for language errors which are common to A2 learners.

LANGUAGE CHECKLIST	✔
Have you used the correct collocations with *business*?	
Have you used the correct tenses?	
Have you used the correct forms of the past simple and the present simple?	
Have you used clauses with *when*?	

8 Make any necessary changes to your paragraph.

OBJECTIVES REVIEW

9 Check your objectives.

I can ...

watch and understand a video about business success.	very well .... not very well
work out meaning from context.	very well .... not very well
add detail to main facts.	very well .... not very well
write a narrative paragraph.	very well .... not very well

WORDLIST

UNIT VOCABULARY		
advertisement (n)	mathematician (n)	employ (v)
advice (n)	occupation (n)	expand (v)
business plan (n)	office (n)	improve (v)
colleague (n)	opportunity (n)	introduce (v)
company (n)	pattern (n)	knit (v)
customer (n)	product (n)	succeed (v)
employee (n)	software (n)	handmade (adj)
fashion designer (n)	success (n)	popular (adj)
goal (n)	wool (n)	successful (adj)
industry (n)		

LEARNING OBJECTIVES

Watch and listen	Watch and understand a video about extraordinary people
Reading skills	Read for detail
Academic writing skills	Write concluding sentences
Writing task	Write an explanatory paragraph

UNL⊘CK YOUR KNOWLEDGE

Look at the photographs and answer the questions below.

1 What are the names of the people?

2 What did they do to become famous?

WATCH AND LISTEN

PREPARING TO WATCH

UNDERSTANDING
KEY VOCABULARY

1 Match the words (1–7) to their definitions (a–g).

1 rescue	a a place that is safe from danger
2 a note	b something bad that happens that is not
3 an accident	wanted or planned, and that hurts someone
4 a refuge	or damages something
5 a leader	c a person who works under the ground,
6 a miner	digging out coal or gold
7 trapped	d a person in control of a group or country
	e save someone from a dangerous situation
	f unable to escape from a place or situation
	g a short letter

PREVIEWING

2 Before you watch, read the newspaper headline and answer the question below.

> ### Chile: Rescue mission starts to save trapped miners

What do you think the video will be about?
a a film
b a competition
c an accident

3 ▶ Watch the video and check your answers.

WHILE WATCHING

UNDERSTANDING
MAIN IDEAS

4 ▶ Watch again. Number the events (a–e) in the correct order.

a The rescue team found a note. _____
b The miners were rescued. _____
c The miners' families came to the mine. _____
d An accident happened in the mine. _____
e The miners were trapped. _____

5 Who did the actions below? Write the actions in the correct place in the table.

1 sent food, water and medicine to the miners
2 gave everyone jobs to do
3 put telephone lines in the mine
4 drew maps of the mine
5 took the men to the refuge
6 sent oxygen into the mine

the miners' leader (Luis Urzúa)	the rescue team

6 ▶ Watch again. Write a number in each gap to complete the sentences below.

1 The accident happened on the _____th August.
2 _____ miners were trapped.
3 The miners were trapped _____ metres underground.
4 The rescue mission started _____ days after the accident.
5 The rescue team got a note from the miners _____ days after the accident.
6 The miners were rescued on the _____th October.
7 The miners were in the mine for _____ days.

7 Why do you think Luis Urzúa came out of the mine after the other men?

DISCUSSION

8 Work with a partner. Discuss the questions below.

1 Do you know of any similar rescues in your country?
2 Should news services bring us good news like the mine rescue? Why? / Why not?

PREPARING TO READ

UNDERSTANDING
KEY VOCABULARY

1 You are going to read a blog. Before you read, look at the sentence below and circle the word (a–c) that is a synonym of the word in bold.

I really **respect** her. She's an excellent teacher.

a dislike
b admire
c employ

2 Match the words (1–7) to their definitions (a–g).

1 a talent   a something special someone can do
2 an operation   b take away
3 cancer   c when doctors cut your body to repair it or to
4 blind   take something out
5 inspire   d amazing
6 incredible   e make other people feel that they want to
7 remove   do good things
                    f unable to see
                    g a disease that makes people very ill

SCANNING TO
PREDICT CONTENT

3 Find and circle the words from Exercise 2 in the blog opposite. What do you think the blog will be about?

a someone who helped people with cancer
b someone who was blind and trained to be a doctor
c someone who was blind but learned how to see

4 Read the blog and check your answers.

WHILE READING

READING FOR
MAIN IDEAS

5 Read the blog again and match the sentences below to the paragraphs (a–d).

1 Ben learned to 'see' again. _____
2 Ben was an ordinary boy but he could do something amazing. _____
3 Ben became a hero for many people. _____
4 Ben became ill and lost his eyes. _____

Respect!

About me
My name is Juliet Selby. I write about people that I admire. I write about a different person every week. Read about their amazing lives here!

Archive
▼ 2013
  ► Ben Underwood
  ► Steve Jobs
  ► Mary Evans
► 2012
► 2011

/2013//Ben Underwood

a Ben Underwood was a normal teenage boy. He loved playing basketball, riding his bicycle, listening to music with his friends and playing video games. But in one way, Ben was different to most other teenagers – he was blind. However, Ben had a special talent. He didn't have any eyes, but he could still see.

b Ben was born in 1992, on 26th January. For the first two years of his life, Ben was a happy and healthy baby. He had a normal life, living with his mother and two older brothers in California. However, when Ben was two years old, his life changed. In 1994, he was taken to hospital because he had problems with his eyes. The doctors looked at his eyes and told his mother the bad news – Ben had cancer. After a few months, he had an operation to remove the cancer. The operation was successful, and Ben was fine. However, the doctors had to remove his eyes and Ben became blind.

c After his operation, Ben developed an incredible talent. When he was three, he learned how to 'see' buildings with his ears. He listened very carefully, and he could hear noises bounce off buildings. The noises told him where the buildings were. Then, when Ben was seven, he learned to 'click'. He made clicking noises with his mouth, and listened for the noises that bounced back from things. In this way, Ben could 'see' where he was and what was around him. This is the same way dolphins see things under water, and bats see in the dark.

d Scientists and doctors were amazed by Ben's talent. There are only a few blind people in the world who can see like Ben. He became famous. He was on TV, and he travelled to different countries and talked to people about his life. Sadly, when Ben was 16, his cancer came back. He died soon after. However, during Ben's life, he taught people that anything is possible. Many people admired him because he inspired them and helped them feel strong. When he died in 2009, over 2,000 people went to his funeral.

6 Read the blog again and write true (T), false (F) or does not say (DNS) next to the statements below.

1 Ben liked playing basketball. _____
2 Ben was just like other teenagers. _____
3 Ben did karate. _____
4 Ben couldn't ride a bicycle. _____
5 Ben was a teenage boy. _____
6 Ben liked writing music. _____

7 Read the blog again and put the events in Ben's life (a–g) in the correct order on the timeline.

a Ben learned how to 'see' buildings with his ears.
b Ben was born.
c Ben learned how to click.
d Ben's cancer came back.
e Ben had a problem with his eyes.
f Ben died.
g Ben went on a TV programme.

```
   1        2        3        4        5        6        7
   |        |        |        |        |        |        |
   +--------+--------+--------+--------+--------+--------+

 _____    _____    _____    _____    _____    _____    _____
```

READING BETWEEN THE LINES

8 Who do you think wrote the blog?

a a scientist   b a journalist

9 Why do you think the author wrote this blog?

a to teach doctors about cancer
b to tell people the story of Ben's life

DISCUSSION

10 Work with a partner. Think of another famous child or teenager and discuss the questions below.

1 What is his/her name and how old is he/she?
2 Why is he/she famous?
3 How are their lives different from other children's or teenagers' lives? Think about the list below.
   • school   • friends
   • hobbies   • home

READING 2

PREPARING TO READ

1 Write the words from the box in the gaps to complete the sentences below.

> former   train   achieve   a dream   a charity

1 _____ is an organization that gives money, food or help to people who need it.
2 We use the word '_____' to describe something that was in the past.
3 You _____ when you practise a sport or exercise to prepare for a competition.
4 _____ is something that you really want to happen in the future.
5 You _____ something when you manage to do something difficult.

WHILE READING

2 Read the blog posts on page 166. Match the sentence halves.

1 Steve Jobs   a looks after her family.
2 Mary Evans   b gave money to charity.
3 The Singapore Women's   c invented a new kind of technology.
  Everest Team   d climbed a mountain.
4 The Salwen family

3 Look at the sentences below. There is one mistake in every sentence. Correct the false information.

a In 2009, the Singapore Women's Everest team climbed Everest after five years of training. _____
b The Salwen family sold their home and gave $600,000 to charities in Ghana. _____
c Steve Jobs died in June 2011. _____
d Mark's mother looks after his grandmother in hospital. _____

Reading for detail

When we read a text, we need to understand the details as well as main ideas. We can locate detail in a text by looking for key words. The key words show us where we can find the information we need. We can then read around the key words to find out more.

/2013//Steve Jobs

a I really admire Steve Jobs, the former CEO of Apple. He invented a new kind of technology. Apple technology is very intelligent but it is also easy to use. The products that he made are also really beautiful. Steve Jobs was an excellent businessman, and he created a successful business in IT. I was very sad when he died in October 2011. I respect him because he changed the way people use technology all over the world.

Ahmed Aziz, _____

/2013//Mary Evans

b My mum, Mary Evans, is a real hero. I have a very big family, with two brothers and three sisters. My mum works very hard every day to look after us, and she is very busy. She always makes time for everyone and she always listens to me if I have a problem.

I have a nephew who is ill and has to go to hospital a lot. My mum often sleeps at the hospital with him. I really respect her because she always looks after my family and makes sure we have everything we need.

Mark Evans, _____

/2013//Singapore Women's Everest Team

c My heroes are the Singapore Women's Everest Team. In 2009, they became the first all-women team to climb Mount Everest. The team of six young women trained for seven years before they climbed the mountain. It was difficult for them to train because Singapore doesn't have any snow, or any mountains. But they didn't stop, and in the end they achieved their goal. They worked hard every day for their dream so I really admire them.

Li Chan, _____

/2013//the Salwen family

d I admire the Salwen family from Atlanta, USA. In 2006, they made a very unusual choice. They decided to sell their house and give half of the money to charity. They moved into a smaller house and gave $800,000 to charities in Ghana. I really respect them because they gave their money to people who needed it.

Jane Kloster, _____

READING BETWEEN THE LINES

MAKING
INFERENCES

4 The jobs of the people writing the comments have been removed. Match the jobs of the authors (1–4) to the paragraphs (a–d).

1 an explorer _____   3 an IT technician _____

2 a teacher _____   4 a charity worker _____

DISCUSSION

5 Work with a partner. Discuss the questions below.

1 Who are the most famous people in your country?

2 How can famous people help charities?

3 Why do news services often write about famous people?

166 READING 2   **UNLOCK** READING AND WRITING SKILLS 2

⊙ LANGUAGE DEVELOPMENT

EXPLANATION

Noun phrases with *of*

In English, we often use the word *of* to join two nouns together and make a noun phrase.

> He is the president of the country.
> He invented a type of technology.
> We write a conclusion at the end of an essay.

1 Match the sentence halves.

1	A chair is	a	the director of the school.
2	I travel to	b	the start of the day.
3	A dog is	c	a kind of furniture.
4	Coffee is	d	a lot of countries.
5	Write your name at	e	a sort of drink.
6	My teacher is	f	the top of the page.
7	We eat breakfast at	g	a type of animal.

ADJECTIVES TO DESCRIBE PEOPLE

2 Are the adjectives in the box positive or negative? Write the words in the correct place in the table.

> reliable   confident   lazy   honest   calm   talented
> kind   shy   intelligent   patient   stupid   clever
> difficult   sensible   selfish   friendly

positive	negative

3 Write adjectives from Exercise 2 in the gaps to complete the sentences.

1 Luka is an _____ person. He always tells the truth.
2 My teacher is _____ . She is very relaxed and doesn't get worried or angry.
3 She always chats to students in other classes. She's so _____ .
4 She doesn't talk very much. She's quite _____ .
5 Ahmed hasn't done anything all day. He's so _____ .
6 James is very _____ . He always comes to work on time and does his job.
7 Ishmael is practical and doesn't do anything stupid. He's very

_____ .

8 He is a very _____ driver. He wins every race easily.

CRITICAL THINKING

At the end of this unit, you will write an explanatory paragraph. Look at this unit's Writing task in the box below.

> Describe a person you admire and explain why.

Putting information in categories

We put things in categories to organize information. Categorizing helps us see similarities and differences between ideas. By putting things in categories, we can also work out what information is relevant and what information is not relevant.

APPLY

1 Work with a partner. Look at the table below. Write the names of three people you admire in each category.

Sports players	Musicians	Business people	Friends/ family	Other

ANALYZE

2 Look at the photographs. Write the person's job under each photograph.

1 _____

2 _____

3 _____

4 _____

3 Read the four reasons below that someone admires the people in Exercise 2. Match the people (1–4) to the reasons (a–d). More than one answer is possible.

    a because they are good at sport _____
    b because they help people   _____
    c because they are clever   _____
    d because they are rich   _____

4 Can you think of other reasons that you might admire somebody? Add your reasons to the list below.

    1 _because they help to change the world_____
    2 _because they give money to people_____
    3 _____
    4 _____

5 Choose a person that you admire from the table in Exercise 1. Why do you admire them?

CREATE

6 Think of four things that this person has done that makes you admire them, and write them in the idea wheel below.

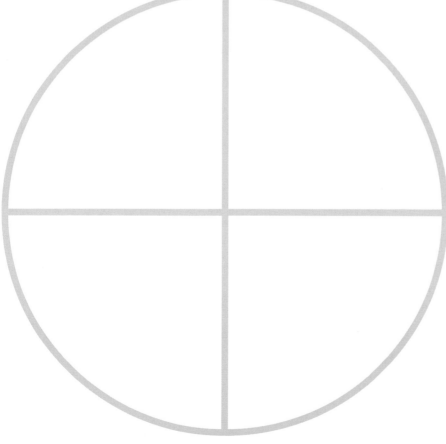

WRITING

GRAMMAR FOR WRITING

Subject and object pronouns

We use subject pronouns to replace nouns or noun phrases that act as the subject of a sentence.

(My father) works hard. (He) owns his own business.

We use object pronouns to replace nouns or noun phrases that act as the object of a sentence.

(The women's football team) are very good. I really admire (them).

We also use object pronouns after prepositions.

The book is about **her**.

subject pronoun	object pronoun
I	me
you	you
he	him
she	her
it	it
we	us
they	them

⟲ **UNLOCK ONLINE**

1 In the sentences below, underline the subject pronouns and circle the object pronouns.

1 She knows them.
2 You don't have it.
3 I don't like her.

4 He can visit us soon.
5 They sent it to her yesterday.
6 We don't know about him.

2 Write the pronouns that can replace the underlined words in each of the sentences below.

1 My team won £1,000. _____
2 They gave a card to my uncle. _____
3 I built my house. _____
4 My grandfather still works every day. _____

UNL○CK READING AND WRITING SKILLS 2

5 She helped <u>her neighbours</u>.   _____
6 <u>His daughter</u> lives in Australia.   _____
7 I talk to <u>my mother</u> every day.   _____
8 He works with <u>my family</u>.   _____

EXPLANATION

Possessive adjectives

Possessive adjectives tell us who or what owns something. We use *my, your, his, her, its, our* and *their* before a noun.

What's **your** number?
Her job is difficult.

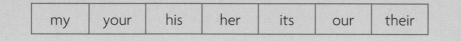

my	your	his	her	its	our	their

3 Circle the correct pronoun to complete the sentences.

1 *My / I* sister works very hard.
2 It is *her / she* bag.
3 Is that *your / you* house?
4 They sold *their / them* house.
5 It is *our / us* blue car.
6 You should write a book about *your / you* life.
7 The computer is slow. *Its / It's* memory is not very good.

ACADEMIC WRITING SKILLS

EXPLANATION

Concluding sentences

The concluding sentence is the last sentence in a paragraph. The concluding sentence gives your opinion or the main ideas in the paragraph. It repeats the main idea of the paragraph using different words.

1 Look at the two sentences and circle the one that is a concluding sentence.

a In conclusion, I admire my mother because she is kind.
b First, she always takes care of my family.

2 Underline the phrase that shows you it is a concluding sentence.

3 What type of punctuation follows the phrase you underlined?

a a full stop
b a comma

4 Match the topic sentences (1–4) to the concluding sentences (a–d).

1 I really admire my teacher.
2 My parents care for my family.
3 Professional footballers have to train every day.
4 My uncle is my hero.

a I admire my uncle a lot.
b It is difficult to be a professional footballer.
c My parents work hard to make sure we have everything we need.
d I respect my teacher because he works hard.

WRITING TASK

> Describe a person you admire and explain why.

PLAN

1 Write a topic sentence to describe the person you are going to write about.

I really admire ...

_____

_____

2 Look at the idea wheel you made in the Critical thinking section (page 169). Write the things in the order you will write about them in your paragraph.

1 _____
_____

2 _____
_____

3 _____
_____

4 _____
_____

3 Write a concluding sentence using *because* to explain why you respect the person.

I respect ... because ...

_____

_____

WRITE A FIRST DRAFT

4 Write the first draft of your paragraph.

5 Use the task checklist to review your paragraph for content and structure.

TASK CHECKLIST	✔
Have you written about someone you admire?	
Have you written about why you respect the person?	
Does your paragraph have a topic sentence, supporting sentences and a concluding sentence?	
Does your concluding sentence give your opinion or repeat the main idea of the paragraph?	

6 Make any necessary changes to your paragraph.

7 Now use the language checklist to edit your paragraph for language errors which are common to A2 learners.

LANGUAGE CHECKLIST	✔
Have you used noun phrases with *of* correctly?	
Have you used adjectives to describe people correctly?	
Have you used subject and object pronouns correctly?	
Have you used possessive adjectives correctly?	

8 Make any necessary changes to your paragraph.

OBJECTIVES REVIEW

9 Check your objectives.

I can ...

watch and understand
a video about
extraordinary people.

very
well

not very
well

read for detail.

very
well

not very
well

write concluding
sentences.

very
well

not very
well

write an explanatory
paragraph.

very
well

not very
well

WORDLIST

UNIT VOCABULARY	
accident (n)	calm (adj)
architecture (n)	clever (adj)
cancer (n)	confident (adj)
charity (n)	difficult (adj)
dream (n)	former (adj)
leader (n)	friendly (adj)
miner (n)	honest (adj)
note (n)	incredible (adj)
operation (n)	intelligent (adj)
refuge (n)	kind (adj)
talent (n)	lazy (adj)
achieve (v)	patient (adj)
inspire (v)	reliable (adj)
remove (v)	selfish (adj)
rescue (v)	sensible (adj)
train (v)	shy (adj)
trap (v)	stupid (adj)
blind (adj)	talented (adj)

LEARNING OBJECTIVES

Watch and listen	Watch and understand a video about space
Reading skills	Scan to find information
Academic writing skills	Organize an essay
Writing task	Write a balanced opinion essay

UNL⊘CK YOUR KNOWLEDGE

1 What do you know about space? Try to answer the questions below.

1 What is the Sun?

   a a star   **b** a planet

2 How long does it take light to travel from the Sun before it gets to the Earth?

   a eight seconds   **b** eight minutes

3 How big is the Moon?

   a 10% of the Earth's size   **b** 25% of the Earth's size

4 What was the first animal in space?

   a a cat   **b** a dog

WATCH AND LISTEN

PREPARING TO WATCH

1 Find the words from the box in the photographs below.

> the solar system   Mars   Earth   the Sun   the Moon
> a star   a galaxy   a telescope

4 _____

5 _____

7 _____

1 _____

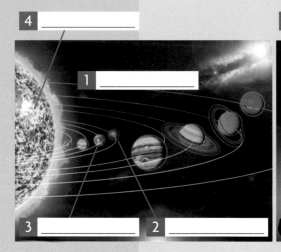

3 _____   **2** _____

8 _____

6 _____

2 Match the words (1–5) to their definitions (a–e).

1	scientist	a	a vehicle used for travelling into space
2	rocket	b	go somewhere new to find out what is there
3	explore	c	a trip from one place to another
4	journey	d	send a spacecraft into the sky
5	launch	e	someone who studies science

WHILE WATCHING

3 ▶ Watch the video. Circle the correct answers to the questions below.

1   When did people first go into space?
    a the late 1900s   **b** the early 1900s
2   Why do we send people and machines into space?
    a to find new places to live   **b** to explore and understand our universe
3   Why did NASA send robots to Mars?
    a to find out if people could live on Mars
    b to find out if there is water on Mars
4   What do scientists study on the International Space Station?
    a how people could live in space   **b** the science of the solar system
5   What does the Hubble telescope take pictures of?
    a the solar system, stars and galaxies   **b** stars, the moon and the sun

4 ▶ Watch again. Put the events in space exploration (1–6) in the correct place on the timeline below.

1959	1969	1990	1997	2005	2020

____   ____   ____   ____   ____   ____

1   The Hubble telescope was sent into space.
2   The USSR sent the first man-made object to the moon.
3   Neil Armstrong walked on the moon.
4   China, Japan, Russia and India to visit the moon?
5   NASA sent the first robots to Mars.
6   The Hubble telescope showed that Pluto has three moons.

5 Write the names of the five countries mentioned in the video.

1 _____   4 _____
2 _____   5 _____
3 _____

6 What do these countries have in common?

DISCUSSION

7 Work with a partner. Discuss the questions.

1   Some organizations now offer private trips into space. Would you like to go into space? Why / Why not?
2   Why are there so many books and films about space?
3   Why don't many countries have a space programme?
4   Is it better for countries or companies to explore space?

READING 1

PREPARING TO READ

1 Before you read, look at the photographs opposite and read the title of the text. Answer the questions below.

1 What do you think the text is about?
   a a book
   b a television programme
2 Where do you think you would find the text?
   a in a magazine
   b in a science text book

2 Read the text and check your answers.

3 Circle the correct definition for the words below.

1 science fiction
   a an academic science report
   b stories about life in the future or in other parts of the universe
2 alien
   a an animal, bird or plant from a planet other than Earth
   b a person you do not like
3 fictional
   a funny
   b imaginary
4 data
   a a particular day or time of the year
   b information or facts about something
5 conditions
   a the situation that something or someone lives in
   b something that will happen in the future
6 a feature
   a an important part of something
   b a time in the past
7 special effects
   a action in films or television programmes created by computers
   b the music in a film or television programme

Alien Planet

Sarah O'Toole

If there is life on another planet, what is it like? This is the question that a new science fiction programme, *Alien Planet*, tries to answer.

In the 94-minute programme, two robots explore a fictional planet. The planet, Darwin IV, is 6.5 light years from Earth. It has two suns, 60% gravity and is smaller and hotter than Earth. It is also home to many alien plants and animals. The robots look at the land and air on the planet, as well as the animals, plants and birds that live there. The robots then send information about the planet to a team of scientists on Earth. The programme is based on the book *Expedition* by Wayne Barlowe.

However, *Alien Planet* is not just normal science fiction, because it is based on real scientific information. A team of designers and scientists described the conditions that would make life possible on Darwin IV. The team then carefully designed the animals and plants that could live in these conditions. The team included famous scientists such as Professor Stephen Hawking, Dr Michio Kaku and Dr James Garvin, the chief scientist at NASA. In the programme, the scientists explain the science behind Darwin IV. They explain why the animals and birds have certain features and discuss the possibility of life on other planets.

Alien Planet is an exciting mix of fact and fiction. The special effects are amazing and the Alien life forms really make the science come alive. I really recommend watching it.

Three alien life forms from *Alien Planet*:

Unth

An Unth is about 2.5 metres tall and has two legs. It runs fast and lives on the ground. It eats plants, and lives and travels in a group. It is brown, with tusks at the front, like an elephant.

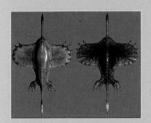

Trunk Sucker

A Trunk Sucker has a long nose and is about 1 metre long. It lives in the forest and drinks the juice from trees. It has wings and flies like a bird.

Daggerwrist

A Daggerwrist is about 2 metres long. It lives in the forest. It jumps from tree to tree like a monkey. It eats other animals.

WHILE READING

4 Read the text (page 181) again and answer the questions below.

1 How long is the programme *Alien Planet*? _____
2 What is the name of the planet in *Alien Planet*? _____
3 Is the planet in *Alien Planet* real? _____
4 What book is *Alien Planet* based on? _____
5 How is *Alien Planet* different from normal science fiction? _____
6 Which famous scientists worked on *Alien Planet*? _____
7 Does the writer think people should watch *Alien Planet*? _____

5 Read the information about the alien life featured on *Alien Planet* and complete the table below.

	Unth	Trunk Sucker	Daggerwrist
How tall/long is it?			
Where does it live?			
What does it eat/ drink?			
What animal is it like?			

Scanning to find information

We often scan the text to find important information. We read the text very quickly and find the key words that give us the information we need.

READING BETWEEN THE LINES

6 The text says that the CGI in *Alien Planet* is amazing. CGI is an abbreviation. What do you think it means?

a Chemistry Group International
b Computer Generated Images
c Centre for General Information

DISCUSSION

7 Work with a partner. Discuss the questions below.

1 Famous scientists took part in the *Alien Planet* programme. Do you think it is a good idea to use science in fictional programmes?
2 Do you think that TV programmes are a good way to teach people about science? Why / Why not?

READING 2

PREPARING TO READ

1 Before you read, match the words (1–7) to their definitions (a–g).

1 wonder	**a** the mix of chemicals in the air around a planet
2 support	**b** the circular journey that a spacecraft or planet makes around a planet
3 atmosphere	
4 evidence	**c** demonstrate that something is true
5 prove	**d** information that shows whether something is true or exists
6 exist	
7 orbit	**e** to be real
	f think about something and try to understand it
	g make an argument stronger

2 Read the title of the text on page 184. What type of text is it?

a a story

b an essay

c a newspaper article

WHILE READING

3 Read the text again and match the main ideas (1–4) to the paragraphs where they are mentioned (A–D).

1 The universe is so big that there must be another planet that has life. _____

2 Earth is the only planet with the right conditions for life. _____

3 There are arguments for and against the idea that life must exist on other planets. _____

4 It is unlikely that there is life on another planet because the conditions for life to exist are too particular. _____

UNLOCK ONLINE

4 In which paragraph does the author do these things?

1 give their own opinion _____

2 talk about arguments for life on other planets _____

3 talk about arguments against life on other planets _____

4 introduce the topic _____

The universe is so big that there must be life on other planets. Discuss the arguments for and against this statement.

A For many years, people have wondered whether we are the only living things in the universe. Some scientists believe that there must be life on other planets because the universe is so big. However, other scientists think that it is very unlikely that there is life on other planets, because planets need a very specific environment for life to start. There are facts that support both sides of the argument.

B On the one hand, the universe is huge. There are billions of stars and thousands of solar systems. Many of these solar systems have planets that go round and round a sun like the Earth. Because there are so many planets in space, it is likely that one of these planets could have the right conditions to have life. Recently, experts using the Kepler telescope found more than 1,200 planets in orbit around a star and 54 of these planets are similar to Earth. Many scientists believe that one of these planets, Kepler 22b, has the right atmosphere and temperature to have life. Even in our solar system, scientists have found evidence of water on Mars and on Titan, one of Saturn's moons. They believe that this could mean that there is, or was, a form of very simple life on these planets.

C On the other hand, a planet needs very particular* conditions to have life. A planet with life would need to have water, the right temperature and the right mix of chemicals in the atmosphere. The Earth has the right conditions to have life, but it is very unlikely that another planet has exactly the same environment as Earth. In addition, although scientists believe that life might exist on other planets, we have never found evidence to prove it. A recent report from Princeton University in the USA suggests that it is very unlikely that there is life on other planets. They believe that we don't have enough scientific evidence to decide if there is life on other planets.

D In conclusion, I do not agree that there is life on other planets. Although the universe is very big, a planet with life needs very special conditions. Earth has exactly the right conditions for life. It is not too hot or too cold. It has water and air and the right chemicals. I do not think that any other planets could have exactly the same conditions as Earth. Therefore, I do not think that there could be life on other planets.

* particular = special

5 Answer the questions below using the information in the text.

SCANNING TO
FIND INFORMATION

1 How many solar systems are there in the universe? _____
2 What is the name of the telescope that has discovered new planets? _____
3 How many planets did the telescope discover that are similar to Earth? _____
4 What is Kepler 22b? _____
5 What did scientists recently discover on Mars? _____
6 What is Titan? _____
7 Which university wrote a report saying that it is unlikely that there is life on other planets? _____
8 What does the report say we need before we can know if there is life on other planets? _____

READING BETWEEN THE LINES

6 Why do you think Kepler 22b is called Kepler 22b?

MAKING
INFERENCES

7 The sentences below are from the text. Which are facts and which are opinions? Write *F* (fact) or *O* (opinion).

1 There must be life on other planets. _____
2 There are billions of stars and thousands of solar systems in the universe. _____
3 It is very unlikely that there is life on other planets. _____
4 A planet needs very specific conditions to have life. _____

DISCUSSION

8 Work with a partner. Discuss the question below.

Space exploration has lead to many inventions. Rank these inventions in order of importance.
a micro computers
b GPS navigation
c satellite TV
d weather forecasts
e electric cars
f robotic arms
g freeze-dried food

⊙ LANGUAGE DEVELOPMENT

GIVING EVIDENCE AND SUPPORTING AN ARGUMENT

1 Match the nouns from the box to the definitions (1–3). One definition has two possible matches.

> studies   reports   research   an expert

1 someone who has a lot of skill in something or a lot of knowledge about something _____
2 documents that tell us about a subject in detail _____
3 the study of a subject to discover new information _____

> In an essay, we have to support our arguments with evidence. We often talk about *research*, *studies* and *reports* to support our arguments. We use the verbs *think* or *believe* for a person, and the verbs *show* or *suggest* for a piece of work.

2 Write the correct verbs from the box above in the sentences. In some sentences, more than one verb is possible.

1 Experts _____ that the moon is too cold for people to live there.
2 Studies _____ that there are over 200 billion stars in the Milky Way.
3 Scientists _____ that we need to study space.
4 Reports _____ that parts of Mars were once covered in ice.
5 Research _____ that there could be 50 billion planets in our galaxy.

should and *it is important to*

In academic writing, we use *should* or *it is important to* to say what we believe is the right or best thing to do.

> It is important to study the science of space.
> We should spend more money on the space programme.

The negative of *should* is *should not*.

> We should not spend more money on the space programme.

3 Which of these things (1–5) should we do in the next 20 years? Use *we should* or *we should not* to write sentences using the phrases below.

1 visit the moon again _____
2 build new rockets _____
3 send robots to other planets _____
4 visit another galaxy _____
5 cancel all space programmes _____

4 Which of these things (1–5) are important to do in the next 20 years? Use *it is important to* to write sentences using the phrases below.

  1 send people into space _____

  2 understand our universe _____

  3 explore other planets _____

  4 find out about stars _____

  5 study the galaxy we live in _____

5 Work with a partner. Compare and discuss your answers.

CRITICAL THINKING

At the end of this unit, you will write a balanced opinion essay. Look at this unit's Writing task in the box below.

> Exploring space is very expensive. Some people think that it is too expensive. However, other people think it is a good way for governments to spend our money. Discuss both points of view and give your opinion.

ANALYZE

1 Look at the essay question above. What is the main topic of the essay?

  a Does it cost too much money to explore space?

  b Does it take too much time to explore space?

  c Is it too difficult to explore space?

2 What is the essay question asking you to do?

  a write instructions

  b write a two-sided opinion essay

  c write a one-sided opinion essay

3 Underline the two points of view in the essay question. Which is for space exploration and which is against space exploration?

4 Is the essay question asking you to include your own opinion? Circle the words that show this instruction.

5 Look at the opinions about a space programme (1–10). Are the arguments *for* or *against* the space programme? Write them in the correct place in the table below.

1 We need to find places to live in space.

2 Other countries have space programmes. We need to compete with them.

3 There's still a lot to explore on Earth. We don't know what is at the bottom of the oceans. Why do we need to go into space?

4 We need to spend money on other things, like helping poor people and fighting disease.

5 We don't need the space programme to develop technology. We can do that in other ways.

6 We need to learn about space to improve what we know about science.

7 We shouldn't waste natural resources on building rockets.

8 We could find things like water, oil or medicine to bring back to Earth.

9 Space programmes aren't important in our daily lives.

10 I would like to go and talk to an alien.

for	against

6 Circle the arguments that are the most convincing.

Evaluating arguments

It is important to think about how good the different arguments about a topic are. Some arguments are stronger than others. We *evaluate* arguments when we decide how strong an argument is. This can help us decide which arguments to include in an essay.

7 Work with a partner. Think of evidence and examples for the arguments you chose in Exercise 6.

CREATE

8 Which opinion below do you agree with most? Explain why.

a We should spend money on exploring space.
b We should not spend money on exploring space.

WRITING

GRAMMAR FOR WRITING

EXPLANATION

Developing sentence structure

We can add phrases to the beginning of a sentence to make a complex sentence.

Some people think that + sentence

Studies show that + sentence

Scientists believe that + sentence

There must be life on other planets. → Some scientists believe that there must be life on other planets.

UNLOCK
ONLINE

1 Put the words in order to make sentences.

1 houses / there will be / by 2050 / on the moon / Scientists believe that /.

_____

2 not a planet / Reports show that / is / Pluto / .

_____

3 a good way to learn about science / TV programmes / are / Some people think that / .

_____

4 Scientists believe that / to study whether people can live in space / need / we / .

_____

5 life / on other planets / Studies suggest that / could exist / .

_____

2 Rewrite the sentences below using the phrases from the explanation box and Exercise 1.

1 It is unlikely that there is life on other planets.
<u>Some people think that it is unlikely that there is life on other planets.</u>

2 Space exploration is important.

_____

3 There are billions of stars in our galaxy.

_____

4 Mars could have life.

_____

5 We need to know more about space.

_____

EXPLANATION

Infinitive of purpose

We can use *to* + infinitive when we want to say why we do something.

NASA sent robots to Mars to find water.

3 Match the sentence halves.

1 We build rockets	**a** to explore it in more detail.
2 We sent the International Space Station into space	**b** to send people into space.
3 We want to land on the moon	**c** to find out if people could live in space.

4 Write in the gaps to complete the sentence below in three different ways.

1 We explore space to _____ .
2 We explore space to _____ .
3 We explore space to _____ .

ACADEMIC WRITING SKILLS

EXPLANATION

Essay organization

An essay is a group of paragraphs about the same topic. Essays are common in academic writing. We write an essay to respond to an essay question.

An essay has an introduction, a main body and a conclusion.

Introduction

↓

Main body

↓

Conclusion

1 Look at the essay in Reading 2 on page 184. Match the parts of the essay (1–3) to the paragraphs (A–D).

1 the introduction _____
2 the main body _____
3 the conclusion _____

2 Look at the essay in Reading 2 again. Match the sentence halves to complete the rules about the structure of a two-sided opinion essay.

1 The introduction of an essay
2 The main body of an essay
3 The conclusion

a gives us more information about the topic.
b summarizes the main ideas of the essay and gives an opinion.
c explains what the essay will be about.

3 Write the words from the box in the gaps to complete the summary about the correct order of paragraphs in an essay.

middle   last   first   one

> The introduction is the ¹_____ paragraph in an essay. The main body is the ²_____ paragraph or paragraphs of the essay. The main body can be ³_____ paragraph or many paragraphs. The conclusion is the ⁴_____ paragraph in an essay.

WRITING TASK

> Exploring space is very expensive. Some people think that it is too expensive. However, other people think it is a good way for governments to spend our money. Discuss both points of view and give your opinion.

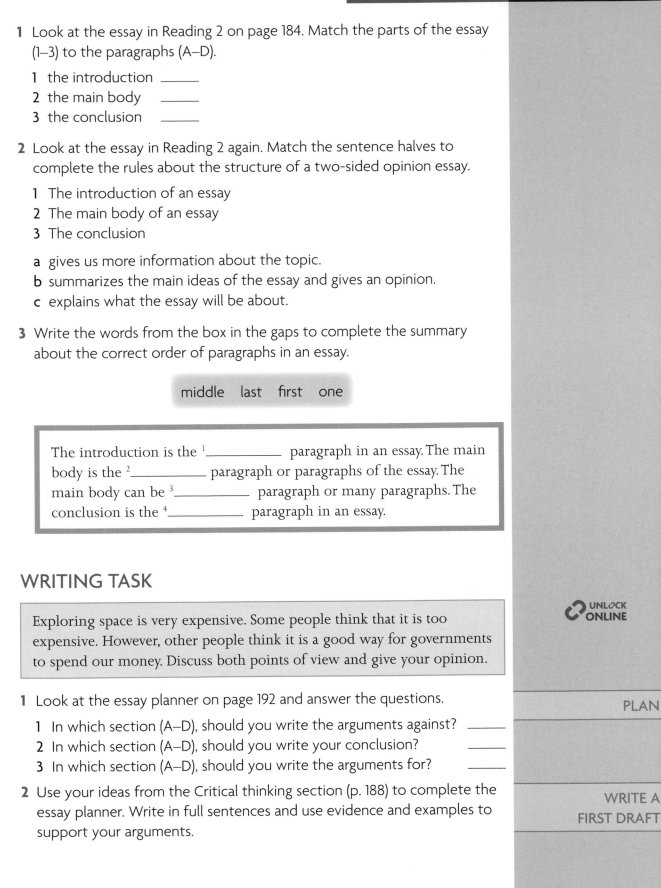 UNLOCK ONLINE

1 Look at the essay planner on page 192 and answer the questions.

PLAN

1 In which section (A–D), should you write the arguments against? _____
2 In which section (A–D), should you write your conclusion? _____
3 In which section (A–D), should you write the arguments for? _____

2 Use your ideas from the Critical thinking section (p. 188) to complete the essay planner. Write in full sentences and use evidence and examples to support your arguments.

WRITE A FIRST DRAFT

A Space exploration is very expensive. Between 1981 and 2011, the US government spent $192 billion on their space programme. Many people believe that space exploration is a waste of money. However, other people think that it is an important and exciting project and that we should spend money on it. This essay will discuss the arguments for and against spending money on space exploration.

B On the one hand, space exploration is important in many ways. _____
_____
_____
_____

C On the other hand, space exploration is very expensive and some people think it is not a useful way to spend money. _____
_____
_____
_____

D In conclusion, I think that we should / should not spend money on space exploration. _____
_____
_____
_____

EDIT

3 Use the task checklist to review your essay for content and structure.

TASK CHECKLIST	✔
Have you included arguments for spending money?	
Have you included arguments against spending money?	
Have you used evidence and examples to support your arguments?	
Have you included your own opinion in the conclusion?	

4 Make any necessary changes to your essay.

5 Now use the language checklist to edit your essay for language errors which are common to A2 learners.

UNLOCK READING AND WRITING SKILLS 2

LANGUAGE CHECKLIST	✔
Have you used the correct vocabulary to give evidence and support your arguments?	
Have you used *should* and *it is important to* correctly?	
Have you used phrases to develop sentence structure?	
Have you used the infinitive of purpose correctly?	

6 Make any necessary changes to your essay.

OBJECTIVES REVIEW

7 Check your objectives.

I can ...

watch and understand a
video about space.

very
well   not very
                                                        well

scan to find information.

very
well   not very
                                                        well

organize an essay.

very
well   not very
                                                        well

write a balanced opinion
essay.   very   not very
                            well   well

WORDLIST

UNIT VOCABULARY			
alien (n)	galaxy (n)	science fiction (n)	telescope (n)
atmosphere (n)	journey (n)	scientist (n)	exist (v)
data (n)	Mars (n)	solar system (n)	explore (v)
Earth (n)	Moon (n)	special effects (n)	launch (v)
evidence (n)	orbit (n)	star (n)	prove (v)
expert (n)	research (n)	Sun (n)	wonder (v)
feature (n)	rocket (n)		

GLOSSARY

Vocabulary	Pronunciation	Part of speech	Definition
UNIT 1			
adjective	/ˈædʒɪktɪv/	(n)	a word that describes a noun or pronoun
beautiful	/ˈbjuːtɪfəl/	(adj)	very attractive or pleasant
boring	/ˈbɔːrɪŋ/	(adj)	not interesting or exciting
cheap	/tʃiːp/	(adj)	costing little money or less than is usual or expected
city	/ˈsɪti/	(n)	a large town
countryside	/ˈkʌntrɪsaɪd/	(n)	land which is not in towns, cities or industrial areas and is either used for farming or left in its natural condition
expensive	/ɪkˈspentsɪv/	(adj)	costing a lot of money
interesting	/ˈɪntrəstɪŋ/	(adj)	someone or something that is interesting keeps your attention because they are unusual, exciting, or have a lot of ideas
modern	/ˈmɒdən/	(adj)	using the newest ideas, design, technology, etc. and not traditional
noisy	/ˈnɔɪzi/	(adj)	making a lot of noise
noun	/naʊn/	(n)	a word that refers to a person, place, thing, event, substance or quality
pollution	/pəˈluːʃən/	(n)	damage caused to water, air, etc. by harmful substances or waste
population	/pɒpjəˈleɪʃən/	(n)	the number of people living in a particular area
rural	/ˈrʊərəl/	(adj)	relating to the countryside and not to towns
traditional	/trəˈdɪʃənəl/	(adj)	following the customs or ways of behaving that have continued in a group of people or society for a long time
traffic	/ˈtræfɪk/	(n)	the cars, trucks, etc. using a road
urban	/ˈɜːbən/	(adj)	belonging or relating to a town or city
verb	/vɜːb/	(n)	a word that is used to say that someone does something or that something happens
UNIT 2			
ancient	/ˈeɪn.ʃənt/	(adj)	of or from a long time ago, having lasted for a very long time
business	/ˈbɪznɪs/	(n)	an organization that sells goods or services
celebrate	/ˈseləbreɪt/	(v)	to do something enjoyable because it is a special day, or because something good has happened
celebration	/seləˈbreɪʃən/	(n)	a special social event, such as a party, when you celebrate something, or the act of celebrating something
company	/ˈkʌmpəni/	(n)	an organization which sells goods or services in order to make money
culture	/ˈkʌltʃə/	(n)	the way of life, especially the habits, traditions and beliefs, of a particular group of people at a particular time
gift	/gɪft/	(n)	a present or something which is given
ground	/graʊnd/	(n)	the surface of the Earth
hang	/hæŋ/	(v)	to fasten or support something at the top leaving the other parts free to move, or to be held in this way
history	/ˈhɪstəri/	(n)	the whole series of events in the past which relate to the development of a country, subject or person
jockey	/ˈdʒɒki/	(n)	a person whose job is riding horses in races
lucky	/ˈlʌki/	(adj)	If an object is lucky, some people believe that it gives you luck.

Vocabulary	Pronunciation	Part of speech	Definition
present	/ˈprezənt/	(n)	something that you give to someone, usually for a particular occasion
relative	/ˈrelətɪv/	(n)	a member of your family
stick	/stɪk/	(n)	a long, thin piece of wood, usually broken or fallen from a tree
successful	/səkˈsesfəl/	(adj)	achieving what you want to achieve
take part	/teɪk ˈpɑːt/	(v)	to be involved in an activity with other people
traditional	/trəˈdɪʃənəl/	(adj)	following the customs or ways of behaving that have continued in a group of people or society for a long time
UNIT 3			
apply	/əˈplaɪ/	(v)	to request something, usually officially, especially by writing or sending in a form
believe	/bɪˈliːv/	(v)	to think that something is true, or that what someone says is true
class	/klɑːs/	(n)	a period of time in which students are taught something
college	/ˈkɒlɪdʒ/	(n)	a place where students are educated when they are between 16 and 18 years old, or after they have finished school
course	/kɔːs/	(n)	a set of classes or a plan of study on a particular subject, usually resulting in an examination or qualification
create	/kriˈeɪt/	(v)	to make something happen or exist
degree	/dɪˈgriː/	(n)	a qualification given for completing a university course
exchange	/ɪksˈtʃeɪndʒ/	(v)	to give something to someone and receive something similar from them
graduate	/ˈgrædjueɪt/	(n)	a person who has finished their school, college or university education
independent	/ˌɪn.dɪˈpen.dənt/	(adj)	not influenced or controlled in any way by other people, events, or things
join	/dʒɔɪn/	(v)	to become a member of a club, group or organization
lecture	/ˈlektʃə/	(n)	a formal talk on a serious or specialist subject given to a group of people, especially students
library	/ˈlaɪbrəri/	(n)	a room or building that contains a collection of books and other written material that you can read or borrow
local	/ˈləʊkəl/	(adj)	relating to an area near you
look after	/lʊk ˈɑːftə/	(v)	to take care of someone or something by keeping them healthy or in a good condition
matter	/ˈmætə/	(v)	to be important, or to affect what happens
notes	/nəʊts/	(n)	information that is written down to help you study, or to help you remember something you are going to write about
office	/ˈɒfɪs/	(n)	a room or building where people work
professional	/prəˈfeʃənəl/	(adj)	Someone is professional if they earn money for a sport or activity which most people do as a hobby.
project	/prəʊˈdʒekt/	(n)	a piece of school work that involves detailed study of a subject
return	/rɪˈtɜːn/	(v)	to go or come back to a place where you were before
similar	/ˈsɪmɪlə/	(adj)	If something or someone is similar to another thing or person, they have many things the same, although they are not exactly the same.
skill	/skɪl/	(n)	an ability to do an activity or job well, especially because you have practised it
student	/ˈstjuːdənt/	(n)	a person who is learning at a college or university, or sometimes at a school

Vocabulary	Pronunciation	Part of speech	Definition
subject	/ˈsʌbdʒɪkt/	(n)	an area of knowledge which is studied in school, college or university
support	/səˈpɔːt/	(v)	to agree with and give encouragement to someone or something because you want them to succeed
teacher	/ˈtiːtʃə/	(n)	someone whose job is to teach in a school or college
train	/treɪn/	(v)	to learn the skills you need to do a job
training	/ˈtreɪnɪŋ/	(n)	the process of learning the skills you need to do a particular job or activity
university	/juːnɪˈvɜːsəti/	(n)	a place where students study at a high level to get a degree
UNIT 4			
blog	/blɒg/	(n)	a record of your activities or opinions that you put on the internet for other people to read and that you change regularly
chat room	/ˈtʃætruːm/	(n)	a place on the internet where you can have discussions with other people
computer program	/kəmˈpjuːtə ˈprəʊgræm/	(n)	a set of instructions that makes a computer do a particular thing
creative	/kriˈeɪtɪv/	(adj)	producing or using original and unusual ideas
disadvantage	/dɪsədˈvɑːntɪdʒ/	(n)	something which makes a situation more difficult, or makes you less likely to succeed
download	/daʊnˈləʊd/	(v)	to copy computer programs, music or other information electronically, especially from the internet or a larger computer
educational	/edʒʊˈkeɪʃənəl/	(adj)	providing education or relating to education
email	/ˈiːmeɪl/	(n)	a message or document sent electronically
email address	/ˈiːmeɪl əˈdres/	(n)	a series of letters, numbers and symbols used to send and receive emails
grade	/greɪd/	(n)	a number or letter that shows how good someone's work or performance is
imagination	/ɪmædʒɪˈneɪʃən/	(n)	the ability to create ideas or pictures in your mind
improve	/ɪmˈpruːv/	(v)	to get better or to make something better
internet banking	/ˈɪntənet bæŋkɪŋ/	(n)	the system that allows you to put in or take out money from a bank account by using the internet
keyboard	/ˈkiːbɔːd/	(n)	a set of keys that you press to use a computer
mobile phone	/ˈməʊbaɪl fəʊn/	(n)	a telephone that you can carry everywhere with you
negative	/ˈnegətɪv/	(adj)	not having enthusiasm or positive opinions about something
online game	/ɒnˈlaɪn geɪm/	(n)	describes a video game that can be bought or used on the internet
overweight	/əʊvəˈweɪt/	(adj)	too heavy or too fat
positive	/ˈpɒzətɪv/	(adj)	feeling enthusiastic and happy about your life and your future
social networking site	/ˈsəʊʃəl ˈnetwɜːkɪŋ saɪt/	(n)	a website that is designed to help people communicate and share information, photographs, etc. with a group
UNIT 5			
alphabet	/ˈælfəbet/	(n)	a set of letters arranged in a fixed order which is used for writing a language
become	/bɪˈkʌm/	(v)	to begin to be something
code	/kəʊd/	(n)	a system of words, letters or signs which is used to represent a message in secret form

Vocabulary	Pronunciation	Part of speech	Definition
complicated	/ˈkɒmplɪkeɪtɪd/	(adj)	involving a lot of different parts, in a way that is difficult to understand
control	/kənˈtrəʊl/	(v)	to make someone or something do what you want
describe	/dɪˈskraɪb/	(v)	to say or write what someone or something is like
develop	/dɪˈveləp/	(v)	to (cause something to) grow or change and become more advanced
explain	/ɪkˈspleɪn/	(v)	to make something clear or easy to understand by giving reasons for it or details about it
extra	/ˈekstrə/	(adj)	more, or more than usual
invent	/ɪnˈvent/	(v)	to design or create something which has never existed before
letter	/ˈletə/	(n)	a symbol that is used in written language and that represents a sound in that language
main	/maɪn/	(adj)	most important or largest
message	/ˈmesɪdʒ/	(n)	a piece of writing or spoken information which one person gives to another
natural	/ˈnætʃərəl/	(adj)	normal or expected
original	/əˈrɪdʒənəl/	(adj)	existing since the beginning, or being the earliest form of something
protect	/prəˈtekt/	(v)	to keep someone or something safe from something dangerous or bad
reason	/ˈriːzən/	(n)	the facts about why something happens or why someone does something
simple	/ˈsɪmpəl/	(adj)	easy to do or to understand
symbol	/ˈsɪmbəl/	(n)	a sign, shape or object which is used to represent something else
text message	/tekst ˈmesɪdʒ/	(n)	a written message, usually containing words with letters left out, sent from one mobile phone to another
type	/taɪp/	(v)	to write something using a keyboard
UNIT 6			
almost	/ˈɔːlməʊst/	(adv)	If something almost happens, it does not happen but it is very close to happening.
careful	/ˈkeəfəl/	(adj)	giving a lot of attention to what you are doing so that you do not have an accident, make a mistake, or damage something
cause	/kɔːz/	(v)	to make something happen, especially something bad
cover	/ˈkʌvə/	(v)	to put something over something else, in order to protect or hide it
damage	/ˈdæmɪdʒ/	(v)	to harm, break or spoil something
dangerous	/ˈdeɪndʒərəs/	(adj)	If someone or something is dangerous, they could harm you.
decide	/dɪˈsaɪd/	(v)	to choose something after thinking about several possibilities
decrease	/dɪˈkriːs/	(n)	a reduction
desert	/ˈdezət/	(n)	a large, hot, dry area of land with very few plants
destroy	/dɪˈstrɔɪ/	(v)	to damage something so badly that it does not exist or cannot be used
drop	/drɒp/	(v)	to fall or to allow something to fall
expert	/ˈekspɜːt/	(n)	someone who has a lot of skill in something or a lot of knowledge of something
fall	/fɔːl/	(v)	to become lower in size, amount or strength
flood	/flʌd/	(n)	a large amount of water covering an area that is usually dry

Vocabulary	Pronunciation	Part of speech	Definition
huge	/hjuːdʒ/	(adj)	extremely large
increase	/ɪnˈkriːs/	(n)	a rise in the amount or size of something
jumper	/dʒʌmpə/	(n)	a piece of clothing usually made of wool which covers the top of your body and is pulled on over your head
last	/lɑːst/	(v)	to be enough for a period of time
lightning	/ˈlaɪtnɪŋ/	(n)	a sudden flash of light in the sky during a storm
maximum	/ˈmæksɪməm/	(adj)	The maximum amount of something is the largest amount that is allowed or possible.
minimum	/ˈmɪnɪməm/	(adj)	The minimum amount of something is the smallest amount that is allowed, needed, or possible.
predict	/prɪˈdɪkt/	(v)	to say that an event or action will happen in the future, especially as a result of knowledge or experience
protect	/prəˈtekt/	(v)	to keep someone or something safe from something dangerous or bad
rainfall	/ˈreɪnfɔːl/	(n)	the amount of rain that falls in a particular place at a particular time
reach	/riːtʃ/	(v)	to get to a particular level, situation, etc.
rise	/raɪz/	(n)	an increase in the level of something
season	/ˈsiːzən/	(n)	a period of the year when a particular thing happens
shock	/ʃɒk/	(n)	a big, unpleasant surprise
signal	/ˈsɪgnəl/	(v)	to make a movement which gives information or tells people what to do
storm	/stɔːm/	(n)	very bad weather with a lot of rain, snow, wind, etc.
survive	/səˈvaɪv/	(v)	to continue to live or exist, especially after almost dying or being destroyed
temperature	/ˈtemprətʃə/	(n)	how hot or cold something is
thunder	/ˈθʌndə/	(n)	the loud noise in the sky that you hear during a storm
tornado	/tɔːˈneɪdəʊ/	(n)	an extremely strong and dangerous wind that blows in a circle and destroys buildings as it moves along
tyre	/taɪə/	(n)	a thick, round piece of rubber filled with air, that fits around a wheel
UNIT 7			
ancient	/ˈeɪntʃənt/	(adj)	from a long time ago
boxing	/bɒksɪŋ/	(n)	a sport in which two competitors fight by hitting each other with their hands
championship	/ˈtʃæm.pi.ən.ʃɪp/	(n)	a high-level competition to decide who is the best, especially in a sport
competitor	/kəmˈpet.ɪ.tər/	(n)	a person, team, or company that is competing against others
crowd	/kraʊd/	(n)	a large group of people who have come together
dream	/driːm/	(n)	something that you want to happen very much but that is not very likely
finally	/ˈfaɪnəli/	(adv)	used especially at the beginning of a sentence to introduce the last point or idea
first	/ˈfɜːst/	(adv)	used to introduce the first idea, reason, etc. in a series
machine	/məˈʃiːn/	(n)	a piece of equipment with several moving parts which uses power to do a particular type of work
major	/ˈmeɪdʒə/	(adj)	more important, bigger or more serious than others of the same type
marathon	/ˈmærəθən/	(n)	a running race of slightly over 26 miles (42.195 kilometres)

Vocabulary	Pronunciation	Part of speech	Definition
race	/reɪs/	(n)	a competition in which people run, ride, drive, etc. against each other in order to see who is the fastest
take place	/ˈteɪk pleɪs/	(v)	to happen
team	/tiːm/	(n)	a group of people who work together to do something
trophy	/ˈtrəʊfi/	(n)	a prize, such as a silver cup, that you get for winning a race or competition
under	/ˈʌndə/	(prep)	below something, or below the surface of something
wrestle	/ˈresəl/	(v)	to fight with someone by holding them and trying to push them to the ground

UNIT 8

Vocabulary	Pronunciation	Part of speech	Definition
advertisement	/ədˈvɜːtɪsmənt/	(n)	a picture, short film, song, etc. which tries to persuade people to buy a product or service
advice	/ədˈvaɪs/	(n)	suggestions about what you think someone should do or how they should do something
business plan	/ˈbɪznɪs plæn/	(n)	a detailed plan describing the future plans of a business
colleague	/ˈkɒliːg/	(n)	someone that you work with
company	/ˈkʌmpəni/	(n)	an organization which sells goods or services in order to make money
employ	/ɪmˈplɔɪ/	(v)	to have someone work or do a job for you and pay them for it
employee	/ɪmˈplɔɪiː/	(n)	someone who is paid to work for someone else
expand	/ɪkˈspænd/	(v)	to increase in size or amount, or to make something increase in this way
fashion designer	/ˈfæʃən dɪˈzaɪnə/	(n)	a person who imagines new kinds of clothes and makes and draws plans for them
goal	/gəʊl/	(n)	an aim or purpose
handmade	/hændˈmeɪd/	(adj)	made by hand instead of by machine
improve	/ɪmˈpruːv/	(v)	to get better or to make something better
industry	/ˈɪndəstri/	(n)	the people and activities involved in one type of business
introduce	/ɪntrəˈdʒuːs/	(v)	to make something exist, happen or be used for the first time
knit	/nɪt/	(v)	to make clothes, etc. by using two long needles to connect wool or another type of thread into joined rows
mathematician	/mæθəməˈtɪʃən/	(n)	someone who studies mathematics
occupation	/ɒkjəˈpeɪʃən/	(n)	your job
office	/ˈɒfɪs/	(n)	a room or building where people work
opportunity	/ɒpəˈtʃuːnəti/	(n)	a situation in which it is possible for you to do something, or a possibility of doing something
pattern	/ˈpætən/	(n)	a design of lines, shapes, colours, etc.
popular	/ˈpɒpjələ/	(adj)	liked by many people
product	/ˈprɒdʌkt/	(n)	something that is made or grown to be sold
software	/ˈsɒftweə/	(n)	programs that you use to make a computer do different things
succeed	/səkˈsiːd/	(v)	to achieve what you are trying to achieve
success	/səkˈses/	(n)	something that has a good result or that is very popular
successful	/səkˈsesfəl/	(adj)	achieving what you want to achieve
wool	/wʊl/	(n)	thick thread or material that is made from the hair of a sheep

Vocabulary	Pronunciation	Part of speech	Definition
UNIT 9			
accident	/'æksɪdənt/	(n)	something bad which happens that is not expected or intended, and which causes injury or damage
achieve	/ə'tʃiːv/	(v)	to succeed in doing something good, usually by working hard
blind	/blaɪnd/	(adj)	not able to see
calm	/kɑːm/	(adj)	relaxed and not worried, frightened, or excited
cancer	/'kæntsə/	(n)	a serious disease that is caused when cells in the body grow in a way that is uncontrolled and not normal
charity	/'tʃærɪti/	(n)	an official organization that gives money, food or help to people who need it, or money, food or help that is given to people who need it
clever	/'klevə/	(adj)	able to learn and understand things quickly and easily
climb	/klaɪm/	(v)	to use your legs, or your legs and hands, to go up or onto the top of something
confident	/'kɒnfɪdənt/	(adj)	certain about your ability to do things well
difficult	/'dɪfɪkəlt/	(adj)	when something is not easy to do or understand
dream	/driːm/	(n)	something that you want to happen very much but that is not very likely
former	/'fɔːmə/	(adj)	happening, existing or true in the past but not now
friendly	/'frendli/	(adj)	behaving in a pleasant, kind way towards someone
honest	/'ɒnɪst/	(adj)	sincere and telling the truth
incredible	/ɪn'kredəbəl/	(adj)	very good, exciting or large
inspire	/ɪn'spaɪə/	(v)	to make someone feel that they want to do something and can do it
intelligent	/ɪn'telɪdʒənt/	(adj)	showing intelligence, or able to learn and understand things easily
kind	/kaɪnd/	(adj)	generous, helpful and thinking about other people's feelings
lazy	/'leɪzi/	(adj)	Someone who is lazy does not like working or using any effort.
leader	/'liːdə/	(n)	a person in control of a group, country or situation
miner	/'maɪnə/	(n)	someone who works in a mine
note	/nəʊt/	(n)	a short letter
operation	/ɒpər'eɪʃən/	(n)	when a doctor cuts someone's body to remove or repair part of it
patient	/'peɪʃənt/	(adj)	having patience
refuge	/'refjuːdʒ/	(n)	protection from danger or unpleasant conditions
reliable	/rɪ'laɪəbəl/	(adj)	able to be trusted or believed
remove	/rɪ'muːv/	(v)	to take something away
rescue	/'reskjuː/	(v)	to save someone from a dangerous or unpleasant situation
selfish	/'selfɪʃ/	(adj)	caring only about yourself and not other people
sensible	/'sentsəbəl/	(adj)	showing good judgment
shy	/ʃaɪ/	(adj)	not confident, especially about meeting or talking to new people
stupid	/'stjuːpɪd/	(adj)	silly or not intelligent
talent	/'tælənt/	(n)	a natural ability to do something
talented	/'tæləntɪd/	(adj)	with talent
train	/treɪn/	(v)	to practise a sport or exercise, often in order to prepare for a sporting event, or to help someone to do this

Vocabulary	Pronunciation	Part of speech	Definition
trap	/træp/	(v)	a dangerous or unpleasant situation which is difficult to escape from

UNIT 10

Vocabulary	Pronunciation	Part of speech	Definition
alien	/ˈeɪliən/	(n)	a creature from another planet
atmosphere	/ˈætməsfɪə/	(n)	the mixture of gases around the Earth
data	/ˈdeɪtə/	(n)	information or facts about something (in scientific English, this can be followed by a plural verb, where the singular form is 'datum')
Earth	/ɜːθ/	(n)	the planet that we live on
evidence	/ˈevɪdənts/	(n)	something that makes you believe that something is true or exists
exist	/ɪgˈzɪst/	(v)	to be present or real
expert	/ˈekspɜːt/	(n)	someone who has a lot of skill in something or a lot of knowledge of something
explore	/ɪkˈsplɔː/	(v)	to go around a place where you have never been in order to find out what is there
feature	/ˈfiːtʃə/	(n)	a typical quality, or an important part of something
galaxy	/ˈgæləksi/	(n)	a very large group of stars held together in the universe
journey	/ˈdʒɜːni/	(n)	when you travel from one place to another
launch	/lɔːntʃ/	(v)	to send a spacecraft or bomb into the sky, or a ship into the water
Mars	/mɑːz/	(n)	the planet that is fourth from the Sun, after the Earth and before Jupiter
Moon	/muːn/	(n)	the round object which moves in the sky around the Earth and can be seen at night
orbit	/ˈɔːbɪt/	(n)	the circular journey that a spacecraft or planet makes around the sun, the moon, or another planet
prove	/pruːv/	(v)	to show that something is true
research	/rɪˈsɜːtʃ/	(n)	when someone studies a subject in detail or tries to find information about a subject
rocket	/ˈrɒkɪt/	(n)	a tube-shaped device containing fuel and an engine that pushes a vehicle into space
science fiction	/ˈsaɪənts ˈfɪkʃən/	(n)	stories about life in the future or in other parts of the universe
scientist	/ˈsaɪəntɪst/	(n)	someone who studies science or works in science
special effects	/ˈspeʃəl ɪˈfekts/	(n)	an unusual type of action in a film, or an entertainment on stage, created by using special equipment
specific	/spəˈsɪfɪk/	(adj)	used to refer to a particular thing and not something general
star	/stɑː/	(n)	a ball of burning gases that you see as a small point of light in the sky at night
sun	/sʌn/	(n)	the large, bright star that shines in the sky during the day and provides light and heat for the Earth, or the light and heat that comes from the sun
telescope	/ˈtelɪskəʊp/	(n)	a piece of equipment, in the shape of a tube, that makes things which are far away look bigger or nearer
the solar system	/ˈsəʊlə ˈsɪstəm/	(n)	the sun and planets that move around it
wonder	/ˈwʌndə/	(v)	to ask yourself questions or express a wish to know about something

UNIT 1 LIFE IN FARAWAY PLACES

Narrator: On mountains, in deserts, in forests and by the sea, in high temperatures and in low temperatures, humans have learnt how to live in every place on Earth. Today, most of us live in urban areas – around 50% of the world's population live in a city. However, in many places, traditional rural life continues in the same way as it has for hundreds of years.

In the far north of Russia, thousands of miles from the capital Moscow, this Khanty village in Siberia is one of the most remote places in the world. Siberia is covered in snow and ice for most of the year. In winter, temperatures here can fall to -53°C. The snow blocks the roads for over 250 days a year. The only way to travel is on skis or on a sledge. This means that life here has developed very differently to the rest of Russia. People have their own traditions and even their own language. They live in small villages and have a quiet, traditional life.

Over 7,000 kilometres away, in Egypt, Siwa is just as remote. Siwa is a small town in the middle of the Sahara desert. Temperatures here can rise to 58°C, so it is too hot for most things to live. However, Siwa is built on an oasis, a series of lakes, which means that people can live here.

For hundreds of years, Siwa was completely isolated and left alone – there were no roads to other towns. This means that, like in Siberia, Siwa has its own language and traditions. Most people use donkeys instead of cars and people speak Siwi, a language spoken only in Siwa. However, recently, a new road has been built, opening Siwa up to the world.

Many people in Siwa are worried that this will change their way of life, and bring new cultures and traditions to the town. Will people in these places be able to keep their traditional way of life? Or will modern life change the way they live forever?

UNIT 2 FESTIVALS: MONGOLIA

Narrator: This is China. Many different groups of people live in this country. Each group has its own history and culture. In northern China is the region of Inner Mongolia. In these thousands of miles of mountains and open grassland, the Mongolian people continue to celebrate their unique culture with the National Holiday.

During the holiday, families stay in traditional tents. They prepare the food and make an open fire. They love to spend time together, eating and telling folk stories. For these people, it is very important to keep their ancient way of life – to keep their culture alive. Horses are at the heart of the Mongolian culture.

The biggest part of the National holiday is the Naadam festival. 'Naadam' means 'games' and the horse races are amazing to watch. Up to a thousand horses take part, and the jockeys show great skill. This is the largest horse race in the world.

In the Mongolian tradition, all the jockeys are children. This is because they are small and the horses can run for longer distances. There are 200 jockeys and they train for months before the race The race starts, and the jockeys run to their horses. They begin to ride across the open grasslands. The jockeys follow the old customs. They do not have seats and they have nothing to hold on to with their feet. This means that the horses are very difficult to ride.

This race is one of the most dangerous in the world. It is a true test of horse-riding skill. And it is a unique example of traditions continuing for hundreds of years. The sun is going down on this year's Naadam festival. Here, on the Mongolian grasslands, the horses will rest until next year.

UNIT 3 A READING CLASS

Narrator: This is a class at a school in the US. The children are all between seven and eight years old. Today, they are having a reading class. Their teacher starts the lesson by reading a story. The teacher wants to train her students to understand texts. In the first part of the lesson, it's important to choose a book that the children will enjoy.

Narrator: The next part of the lesson is called 'independent reading'. This means that the children work alone, without help. The teacher asks the children to read a book on their own. The students choose a book and read it. They make notes about what is in their text. For example, is it similar to another text they have read before? Or is it similar to something in real life?

Students read and make a connection with things in their own life. The teacher goes round the class and sits with her students. She gives help and support, and talks with them about the notes they made. At the end of independent reading, the teacher asks the class to discuss what they read.

Narrator: The teacher asks different students to talk about their ideas with the rest of the class.

Child: Now Fudge, Peter and their dad are on the train going to Washington and Fudge keeps on asking if he can go to the café car and my sister always does that to me when we're going to Washington on the train.

Teacher: You're constantly making connections. You're always thinking about the things in your life and how they connect to the things in your story.

Narrator: The teacher wants to help her students to become independent: to work things out on their own. And, hopefully, the children will learn to love reading, too.

UNIT 4 THE RISE OF SOCIAL MEDIA

Narrator: Facebook, MySpace, Twitter, YouTube. Today, social media is a huge part of most people's lives, and websites like these have changed the way we communicate. Even if you are too busy to phone or visit someone, it is easy to find time to send them a message online. Social networks make it easy to keep in touch with lots of people, and we have more friends than ever before.

With social media, we can share the videos, websites and music we like online. This means that we now have more control over what we watch, read and listen to. Blogs also mean that we can read articles about everything from news to fashion to food, written by all kinds of different people all over the world. This is very different from traditional media, like newspapers, magazines or TV.

The social networking site Facebook was started by Mark Zuckerberg in 2004. It is now one of the biggest businesses in the world. More than five hundred and twenty million people use the website every day: looking at profiles, talking to their friends and uploading photos.

Zuckerberg: It started off pretty small, right. We threw together the first version of the product in just a week and a half. Two thirds of Harvard students were using it within a couple of weeks. And then we expanded to all the colleges in the US, then all the high schools, then a lot of companies and then we made it so that anyone can sign up. And since then, it's grown from about ten million active users to maybe 50. It's still growing at this rate where it doubles every six months.

Narrator: But the online world changes quickly. Who knows what will be the next big thing?

UNIT 5 THE IMPORTANCE OF CODES

Narrator: A code is a secret language – a useful way to share secret information between certain people and make sure that other people can't understand it. People have used codes throughout history.

About 2,000 years ago, the Romans, for example, used simple codes to share secret messages. In one code, the Romans changed one letter from the alphabet for a different one. Roman soldiers also used pots of water to send messages over long distances. Every pot of water had the same list of messages inside. When soldiers saw a light, they started to pour the water out of the pot. When they saw a second light, they stopped. This meant that all the soldiers saw the same message at the same time. In the 1900s, codes became much more complicated – and so did breaking them!

In 1919, a new type of code machine, called the Enigma machine, was invented. The Enigma machine looked like a typewriter. But when someone typed a message, it automatically became a code. The amazing thing about it is the number of codes.

There were billions of possible codes, so it was very difficult to understand the original message. The mathematicians who worked with the Enigma machines helped to develop the first computers.

Today, codes have become part of our everyday lives. Computers, mobile phones and the internet all need codes to work. For example, when we send emails and credit card payments online, codes protect our personal information. Today, modern technology means that codes are part of our everyday lives. Codes have a long history and they are now more important than ever.

UNIT 6 STORMCHASERS

Narrator: Tornadoes are the most violent storms on the planet. They happen all over the world but most are found in Tornado Alley, in the middle of the United States – especially in north Texas, Kansas, Nebraska and Oklahoma. Most tornadoes are less than 80 metres wide and have a wind speed of less than 180 kilometres an hour. But some tornadoes are more than three kilometres wide and have a wind speed of 500 kilometres per hour. These tornadoes are huge and extremely dangerous. They destroy houses, trees, buildings and cars, and they can even kill. In 2011, during the worst tornado season in the US since 1950, 551 people were killed by tornadoes.

When people hear tornado sirens, they normally run for cover. But not everybody runs away. Stormchasers actually follow the tornadoes. Stormchasers follow the storms to get scientific facts about how tornadoes work.

Josh Wurman is a scientist. He is a professional stormchaser – his job is to study tornadoes. He has a large team and uses advanced technology to get information about the tornadoes. This radar helps track the tornado. He even has a specially protected truck that can go right inside the storms.

Other stormchasers follow the storms to take pictures and videos. Reed Timmer works from home. He works with a few friends and uses the internet, a video camera and a 4x4 car to follow tornadoes. He makes money by selling the videos of storms to television companies. The stormchasers' job is very dangerous, but it is also very important. The pictures and information they get help us understand tornadoes better. By improving our understanding of tornadoes, we can predict the storms and hopefully save lives in the future.

UNIT 7 SPORTS AND COMPETITION

Narrator: This is the story of an ordinary girl from Italy with a great dream. This is Marika Diana. She's a 17-year-old schoolgirl who dreams of racing cars. She is too young to have a normal driving licence, but she is already one of the fastest race-car drivers in Italy. She wants to be the first woman to win the national championships.

Narrator: Marika began racing in go-karts when she was seven years old. Now she trains every week. Nearly every Formula One champion started this way. Marika has her big race tomorrow. Will her dream come true?

Motor sports started over 100 years ago, and today it is one of the most popular sports in Italy. In this race, Marika will reach a speed of 220 kilometres an hour. Her car will be only five centimetres above the ground. It is dangerous, and Marika knows it. She won the last three races. Now, she needs to be in the top three places to win the national championship.

Narrator: The race begins. Another car overtakes Marika. Other drivers try to pass her, but Marika does not give up. Her family support her all the way. She crosses the finish line in second place. Marika didn't win the race, but she becomes the first woman to win Italy's national championship.

Marika: It's a passion that I believe I have in my veins: in my blood. It's something that comes from inside.

Narrator: It's a great day for Marika.

UNIT 8 THE CHANGING WORLD OF BUSINESS

Narrator: In business, it is important for a company to change, or adapt, as the world changes. These changes are often linked to technology – or the way people live their lives. Let's look at three good examples of companies that do this.

EA Games is one of the biggest video game companies in the world. Because video games are linked with technology, business in this area changes very quickly.

Since the first popular computer game *Pong* was made, in 1972, computer graphics have improved a lot.

Another company that keeps moving is Ferrari. The competitive world of Formula One means that Ferrari has to improve all the time to win more races. They use some of the new technology from their Formula One cars in their road cars, which sell for hundreds of thousands of pounds. One thing that doesn't change is how popular the Italian company is around the world – and they don't even make advertisements.

The fashion designer and entrepreneur Jhane Barnes also knows how important new ideas are in business. In the early 1990s, she met a mathematician called Bill Jones. He had made a computer program that created new patterns using maths. Barnes thought this was a great opportunity and the two worked together. They used what they knew about fashion, maths and technology to make completely new designs.

EA, Ferrari and Jhane Barnes are three very different companies in three very different industries. But, they all show that, in business, you have to change and adapt to be a success.

UNIT 9 MINE RESCUE

Narrator: Northern Chile on the 5th of August 2010. In the Copiapo mine, it was a normal day for the miner Luis Urzúa and his team. Then, disaster. The mine collapsed. There was no way out. Thirty-three miners were trapped inside, 700 metres under the desert. The miners' families hurried to the mine. They built a camp outside, where they waited for news.

Four days later, the rescue mission began. The rescue team didn't know where the miners were. They used drills to make holes in the mine and find where the trapped men were. On day seventeen, they pulled up one of the drills. It had a note in it. The note said: 'We are inside the refuge and well, all thirty-three of us'. The rescue mission used metal pipes to send food, water and medicine to the miners. They sent oxygen into the mines so the miners could breathe. They also sent telephone lines so the miners could talk to their families.

Deep under the ground, Luis Urzúa became the miners' leader. Luis Urzúa took the men to the refuge, and organized the group. He gave everyone jobs to do, and made sure they had food and water. He also drew maps of the mine to send to the rescue team. The men said that Luis was calm, funny and organized, which made him a good leader.

The miners were rescued on the 13th of October 2010. They were all fine. They had been underground for 69 days. This is the longest time anyone has ever been trapped in a mine and survived. Luis Urzúa was the last man out. The president was waiting for him outside the mine. He said: 'You have been a very good boss and leader. Now go and hug your family.'

The Copiapo mine is now closed. The government is going to build a museum and a monument for the miners.

UNIT 10 OUR JOURNEY INTO SPACE

Narrator: People have been interested in space since the beginning of time. But it was not until rockets were invented in the late 1900s that people could begin to explore space themselves.

We now send both humans and machines into space to explore and understand the universe we live in.

In 1959, the USSR sent the first man-made object to the moon. Then, in 1969, Neil Armstrong became the first man to walk on the moon.

Today, China, Japan, Russia and India are all planning to visit the moon by 2020. In 1997, NASA sent robots to Mars – to explore and find out if the planet had water or not. Why are they looking for water? Because water could mean that there is, or once was, life on Mars. But space exploration is not just about sending people to other planets.

On the International Space Station, the largest man-made object in the sky, scientists are studying what it would be like for people to live in space. Six scientists live on the ISS, 24 hours a day, 365 days a year, looking at how we could eat, sleep and live in space.

The pictures from the Hubble telescope give us important information about the universe – from the solar system, to stars, galaxies and asteroids. Since the telescope was launched in 1990, we have learnt about how stars are born and die, and how galaxies are formed.

In 2005, the Hubble telescope showed that Pluto has three moons, instead of one, as we thought before. Who knows what amazing things we might find as we continue our adventure into space?

ACKNOWLEDGEMENTS

Author acknowledgements

I would like to thank my editors Rhona Snelling, Celia Warin and Frances Disken for their advice, support and patience during the writing of this text. I would also like to thank my wife, Megumi Harada O'Neill, for providing an invaluable learner's perspective on many of the activities and explanations in the book.

Richard O'Neill

Publisher's acknowledgements

The publishers are extremely grateful to the following people and their students for reviewing and trialling this course during its development. The course has benefited hugely from your insightful comments, advice and feedback.

Mr M.K. Adjibade, King Saud University, Saudi Arabia; Canan Aktug, Bursa Technical University, Turkey; Olwyn Alexander, Heriot Watt University, UK; Valerie Anisy, Damman University, Saudi Arabia; Anwar Al-Fetlawi, University of Sharjah, UAE; Laila Al-Qadhi, Kuwait University, Kuwait; Tahani Al-Taha, University of Dubai, UAE; Ozlem Atalay, Middle East Technical University, Turkey; Seda Merter Ataygul, Bursa Technical University Turkey; Harika Altug, Bogazici University, Turkey; Kwab Asare, University of Westminster, UK; Erdogan Bada, Cukurova University, Turkey; Cem Balcikanli, Gazi University, Turkey; Gaye Bayri, Anadolu University, Turkey; Meher Ben Lakhdar, Sohar University, Oman; Emma Biss, Girne American University, UK; Dogan Bulut, Meliksah University, Turkey; Sinem Bur, TED University, Turkey; Alison Chisholm, University of Sussex, UK; Dr. Panidnad Chulerk , Rangsit University, Thailand; Sedat Cilingir, Bilgi University, Istanbul, Turkey; Sarah Clark, Nottingham Trent International College, UK; Elaine Cockerham, Higher College of Technology, Muscat, Oman; Asli Derin, Bilgi University, Turkey; Steven Douglass, University of Sunderland, UK; Jacqueline Einer, Sabanci University, Turkey; Basak Erel, Anadolu University, Turkey; Hande Lena Erol, Piri Reis Maritime University, Turkey; Gulseren Eyuboglu, Ozyegin University, Turkey; Muge Gencer, Kemerburgaz University, Turkey; Jeff Gibbons, King Fahed University of Petroleum and Minerals, Saudi Arabia; Maxine Gilway, Bristol University, UK; Dr Christina Gitsaki, HCT, Dubai Men's College, UAE; Sam Fenwick, Sohar University, Oman; Peter Frey, International House, Doha, Qatar; Neil Harris, Swansea University, UK; Vicki Hayden, College of the North Atlantic, Qatar; Joud Jabri-Pickett, United Arab Emirates University, Al Ain, UAE; Aysel Kilic, Anadolu University, Turkey; Ali Kimav, Anadolu University, Turkey; Bahar Kiziltunali, Izmir University of Economics, Turkey; Kamil Koc, Ozel Kasimoglu Coskun Lisesi, Turkey; Ipek Korman-Tezcan, Yeditepe University, Turkey; Philip Lodge, Dubai Men's College, UAE; Iain Mackie, Al Rowdah University, Abu Dhabi, UAE; Katherine Mansfield, University of Westminster, UK; Kassim Mastan, King Saud University, Saudi Arabia; Elspeth McConnell, Newham College, UK; Lauriel Mehdi, American University of Sharjah, UAE; Dorando Mirkin-Dick, Bell International Institute, UK; Dr Sita Musigrungsi, Prince of Songkla University, Hatyai, Thailand; Mark Neville, Al Hosn University, Abu Dhabi, UAE; Shirley Norton, London School of English, UK; James Openshaw, British Study Centres, UK; Hale Ottolini, Mugla Sitki Kocman University, Turkey; David Palmer, University of Dubai, UAE; Michael Pazinas, United Arab Emirates University, UAE; Troy Priest, Zayed University, UAE; Alison Ramage Patterson, Jeddah, Saudi Arabia; Paul Rogers, Qatar Skills Academy, Qatar; Josh Round, Saint George International, UK; Harika Saglicak, Bogazici University, Turkey; Asli Saracoglu, Isik University, Turkey; Neil Sarkar, Ealing, Hammersmith and West London College, UK; Nancy Shepherd, Bahrain University, Bahrain; Jonathan Smith, Sabanci University, Turkey; Peter Smith, United Arab Emirates University, UAE; Adem Soruc, Fatih University Istanbul, Turkey; Dr Peter Stanfield, HCT, Madinat Zayed & Ruwais Colleges, UAE; Maria Agata Szczerbik, United Arab Emirates University, Al Ain, UAE; Burcu Tezcan-Unal, Bilgi University, Turkey; Dr Nakonthep Tipayasuparat, Rangsit University, Thailand; Scott Thornbury, The New School, New York, USA; Susan Toth, HCT, Dubai Men's Campus, Dubai, UAE; Melin Unal, Ege University, Izmir, Turkey; Aylin Unaldi, Bogaziçi University, Turkey; Colleen Wackrow, Princess Nourah bint Abdulrahman University, Riyadh, Saudi Arabia; Gordon Watts, Study Group, Brighton UK; Po Leng Wendelkin, INTO at University of East Anglia, UK; Halime Yildiz, Bilkent University, Ankara, Turkey; Ferhat Yilmaz, Kahramanmaras Sutcu Imam University, Turkey.

Special thanks to Peter Lucantoni for sharing his expertise, both pedagogical and cultural.

Text and Photo acknowledgements

The authors and publishers acknowledge the following sources of copyright material and are grateful for the permissions granted. While every effort has been made, it has not always been possible to identify the sources of all the material used, or to trace all copyright holders. If any omissions are brought to our notice, we will be happy to include the appropriate acknowledgements on reprinting.

p.12: (1) © Eric Limon/Shutterstock; p.12: (2) © szefai/Shutterstock; p.12: (3) © Steven Vidler/Eurasia Press/Corbis; pp.14/15: © Steven Vidler/Eurasia Press/Corbis; p.22(B): © Zubin Shroft/Getty Images; p.22(T): © Andrew Bret Wallis/Getty Images; p.28: © Tiber Bognar/AgeFotostock/Corbis; p.33(C): © Rich-Joseph Farun; p.33(L):© Kimikong/Getty Images; pp.32/33: epa/Alamy; p.33(R): © Jim Hughes/Corbis; p.37(T): © Anderson Ross/Corbis; p.37(CR): Fotosearch/Superstock; p.37(CL): © Stacey Barnett/Shutterstock; p.37(B): © Terry Harris/Alamy; p.37(BR):AFP/Getty Images; p.39(B&T): © John Elk III/Alamy; p.50/51: © Martin Mayer/Alamy; p.50(L): Cultura Creative/Alamy; p.50(R): © Phil Boorman/Corbis; p.55: © Andy Rain/Corbis; p58(CL): © Kevin Dodge/Corbis; p58(CR): iStockphoto/Thinkstock; p58(T): © Randy Faris/Corbis; p.58(B): Design Pics/Thinkstock; pp.69/70: © R Hamilton Smith/AgStock Images; p.70(CL): Photo Edit/Alamy; p.70(CL&BR): © Invar Bjork/Alamy; p70(TR): PSL Images/Alamy; p.73(L): Radius Im ages/Alamy; p.73(TR): Blend Images/Alamy; pp.86/87: © Illia Torlin/Shutterstock; p.86(TL): Piyato/Shutterstock; p.86(TC): Kaspri/Shutterstock; p.86(TR): © Christophe Testi/Shutterstock; p.86(BL): Arcady/Shutterstock; p.86(BC): © Robert J Byers II/Shutterstock; p.86(BR): © Dragana Gerasimoski/Shutterstock; p.92: © Rain Chen/Shutterstock; pp.104/105: © Sebastian Opitz/Corbis; p.105(TL): © Bryan Mullennix/Getty Images; p.105(TR): © Frans Lanting/Corbis; p.105(BL): © Christophe Boisvieux/Hemis/Corbis; p.105(BR): © Andre Gallant/Getty Images; pp.122/123: © Walter Bieri/Corbis; p.127: © James Montgomery/Corbis; p.130: epa/Alamy; p.140: © Pavel L Photo & Video/Shutterstock; p.141(L): © Michael Kappelar/Corbis; p.141(R): © Getty Images; p.149: © Bartoz Hadyniak/Getty Images; pp.158/159: ©Christian Liewig/Tem Sport/Corbis; p.158(C): Allstar Picture Library/Alamy; p.158(R): © Tim Graham/Getty Images; p.163: MCT/Getty Images; p.168(L): MBI/Alamy; p.168(TC): Monkey Business Images/Shutterstock; p.168(B): ©Tom Grill/Corbis; p.168(R): © Yuri Arcurs/Shutterstock; pp.176/177: NASA/Science Photo Library; p.178(TR): © Joes Antonio Penas/Science Photo Library; p.178(L): © Larry Landolfi/Science Photo Library; p.178(BR): © Roger Gendler/Science Photo Library; p.181(All): © Discovery Communications LLC 2013; p.181: *Aliens: Is Anybody Out There?* Cambridge Discovery Education ™ Interactive Readers © Cambridge University Press 2014.

All videos stills by kind permission of © Discovery Communications LLC 2014

Corpus

Development of this publication has made use of the Cambridge English Corpus (CEC). The CEC is a multi-billion word computer database of contemporary spoken and written English. It includes British English, American English and other varieties of English. It also includes the Cambridge Learner Corpus, developed in collaboration with Cambridge English Language Assessment.

Dictionary

Cambridge dictionaries are the world's most widely used dictionaries for learners of English. Available at three levels (Cambridge Essential English Dictionary, Cambridge Learner's Dictionary and Cambridge Advanced Learner's Dictionary), they provide easy-to-understand definitions, example sentences, and help in avoiding typical mistakes. The dictionaries are also available online at dictionary.cambridge.org. © Cambridge University Press, reproduced with permission.

Illustrations

Ricky Capanni (HL Studios) pp114, 115; Fiona Gowen pp130 (map), 132, 133, 134; Ben Hasler (NB Illustration) pp130 (nettle), 136; Oxford Designers & Illustrators pp90, 91

Picture research by Alison Prior

Typeset by emc design ltd